DIVINE
INVASIONS

Other Books by Dr. Robert Jeffress

Not All Roads Lead to Heaven

A Place Called Heaven

Courageous

Invincible

What Every Christian Should Know

18 Minutes with Jesus

The 10

Are We Living in the End Times?

Jesus Revealed in the End Times

DIVINE INVASIONS

Experience God's Miracles in Your Life Today

DR. ROBERT JEFFRESS

BakerBooks
a division of Baker Publishing Group
Grand Rapids, Michigan

Published by Baker Books
a division of Baker Publishing Group
Grand Rapids, Michigan
BakerBooks.com

Printed in the United States of America

Library of Congress Cataloging-in-Publication Data
Names: Jeffress, Robert, 1955– author
Title: Divine invasions : experience God's miracles in your life today / Dr. Robert Jeffress.
Description: Grand Rapids, Michigan : Baker Books, a division of Baker Publishing Group, [2026] | Includes biographical information. | Includes bibliographical references.
Identifiers: LCCN 2025046860 | ISBN 9781540904430 cloth | ISBN 9781493456543 ebook
Subjects: LCSH: Miracles | Providence and government of God—Christianity | Christian life
Classification: LCC BT97.3 .J44 2026
LC record available at https://lccn.loc.gov/2025046860

All italics in direct Scripture quotations are the author's emphasis.

Some names and details have been changed to protect the privacy of the individuals involved.

This work was created without the use of any generative artificial intelligence (AI) or machine learning tools, and its content is original to the human author(s).

Cover design by Peter Gloege, Look Design Studio

Published in association with Yates & Yates, www.yates2.com.

Baker Publishing Group publications use paper produced from sustainable forestry practices and postconsumer waste whenever possible.

26 27 28 29 30 31 32 7 6 5 4 3 2 1

To Shane and Elizabeth Lewis, who have been the recipients of God's divine invasion. Thank you for your faithfulness in spreading His Word through *Pathway to Victory*.

CONTENTS

CHAPTER 1

DIVINE INVASIONS

THE DAY OF MY FATHER'S FUNERAL was the day I almost died.

My siblings and I were still grieving the untimely death of our mother from cancer when our father was diagnosed with the same dreaded disease. Just four short years later, we gathered again in a little cemetery in Van Alstyne, Texas, to bury him next to our mom.

The afternoon of my father's graveside service was dismal, with a steady rainfall that mirrored our tears. After we concluded our remembrances, the funeral director drove Amy (my wife) and me, my brother and sister, and my stepmother to my father's home in Richardson. I sat on the passenger side, watching the limousine's windshield wipers struggle to keep up with the blinding rain. As the funeral director prepared to turn left onto my father's street, I was only half listening to him discuss the ups and downs of the burial business when I noticed that he proceeded into the intersection on an unprotected yellow arrow. Instinctively, I looked to my right. A large Cadillac sedan was barreling down on us. I screamed, "Don, no!" My family shrieked and braced for impact.

Then everything went into slow motion.

Two thoughts flashed across my mind: *I'm about to die with some of the people I love most*, quickly followed by, *Isn't it ironic that I'm going to die on the day of my father's funeral?*

But I didn't.

I have no natural explanation for how the Cadillac, which didn't slow and was heading straight toward us, missed our limousine on that rain-slick road. I can only attribute our survival to the supernatural—that God miraculously protected my family members from more grief on that already grief-filled day.

This is just one of several times God has miraculously intervened in my life and the lives of my loved ones. I refer to these occurrences as "divine invasions"—milestone moments of supernatural power, protection, provision, or healing with no other explanation except for the movement of God.

Divine invasions like these don't happen often. After all, the word *supernatural* means "beyond or above that which is natural." The reason we say something is *super*natural is that it is not a regular occurrence in our natural lives; it's rare. Yet I can point to some truly supernatural events in my life that confirm to me the reality of an invisible God. And in almost fifty years as a pastor, I've heard countless other stories of God invading people's lives in ways that can only be described as miraculous.

Does God Still Work Miracles Today?

Whenever we talk about miracles, we tend to think about God's acts of parting the Red Sea, feeding twenty-five thousand people with five loaves and two fish, healing the lame, or raising the dead. We read stories like that in Scripture and think, *Well, that's a nice Bible story. God dramatically intervened back in those days, but we can't depend upon God to do the same things in our lives today. After all, times have changed.*

Is that true? Has God just left us on our own, and we shouldn't expect His supernatural answers to our prayers or miraculous interventions in the world anymore? When it comes to the subject of miracles, there are different perspectives among Christians.

On one extreme, the theological tradition called *cessationism* claims that the sign gifts—the gifts of speaking in tongues, healing, and prophecy—stopped in the first century, after the Scriptures were completed and the prophets and apostles passed from the scene. According to this view, God quit working miraculously in our world because there is no longer any need to authenticate a person's message as being from God by the miraculous signs he or she performs. The Bible is the standard by which we judge the authenticity of a person's message today.

The other extreme perspective is called *continuationism*, which teaches that miracles happen today in the very same way that they happened during New Testament times. Christians who hold this view say the sign gifts, including miracles, were not given only in the first century to authenticate the apostles to the early church. Rather, all the sign gifts continue today in the exact same way to authenticate a person's ministry and teaching as coming from God, as well as to meet the needs of God's people.

So, which is it? Is God still intervening miraculously in the world and in your life, or are the days of miracles over?

As we consider this question, it's important to keep in mind that when an issue isn't black-and-white in the Scriptures, it falls into the category of "nonessentials." There are some doctrinal issues that are clear in the Bible that we must agree on, such as the deity of Jesus Christ and salvation by faith alone. These doctrines are "essentials," and they are important to our eternal relationship with God.

The question of whether sign gifts have ceased is a nonessential issue, along with other issues like our particular view about the age of the earth or the end times. Someone has said, "In the essentials, unity. In the nonessentials, liberty. In all things, charity." So, when it comes to secondary (nonessential) issues, including the issue of miracles that we're going to look at in this book, there's great space for diversity in the body of Christ.

Is God still intervening miraculously in the world and in your life, or are the days of miracles over?

However, just because the issue of miracles isn't an *essential* belief of Christianity doesn't mean it's not an *important* belief. When you face a problem, you need to know, *Can I go to God and ask Him to divinely intervene in my situation, or am I wasting my time?* What you believe about miracles affects how you pray and how you live.

With that said, I'll share with you my personal view of miracles. As a seminary student and young pastor, I held the belief that miracles have ceased. However, after almost five decades of ministry, I have experienced and seen far too many things both here in America and around the world that can only be explained by the supernatural movement of God. I don't think we should put God in a box and say God cannot do this or that anymore. But I also don't think we should go any further than Scripture does. The Bible does not say that God is out of the miracle business.

My personal belief now is that God still performs miracles today. His power to work miracles has not changed. The same God who miraculously intervened time and time again in the Bible is available to intervene in your life and mine. I believe God still heals people physically. I believe God could choose to raise people from the dead, especially in those parts of the world where there is no Bible. I am convinced that God is still in the miracle-working business.

In my opinion, what has changed since the days of the New Testament is that God no longer uses human beings to act as intermediaries between Himself and those for whom He wants to perform a miracle. God can and does work miracles today if He so chooses; He's just eliminated the need for a middleman.

I agree with something my predecessor at First Baptist Church of Dallas, Dr. W. A. Criswell, used to say: "I believe in divine healing. I just don't believe in divine healers."[1] Because we have the New Testament, we no longer need miracles to authenticate genuine prophets of God. Nor do we need miracles as a sign to validate the ministry of preachers today, since faithfulness to the Word of God is a sufficient measuring stick. So if God wants to heal somebody today, He does it directly. God can work miracles at any time and in any way He wants. There's no reason for Him to use an intermediary. We should pray for miracles and ask God to accomplish them in His way and His time.

That's what we're going to examine in this book: Should we expect to experience God's miracles in our lives today, and if so, how does God divinely invade our lives? I felt compelled to write this book because I've seen and talked with far too many Christians who are struggling with difficult circumstances and are starting to give up hope. Perhaps you have a great need in your life, but you're afraid to ask God for a miracle because you don't really believe He will intervene—and you don't want to be disappointed. Or maybe you've decided that your painful situation is too much for God to handle and have stopped praying for a miracle.

Because we live in a world of material substance, we need some assurances along the way that our faith is real, that there really is a spiritual realm out there, and that there really is a God who hears and answers our prayers for divine intervention. And that's why, occasionally, we need milestone encounters with the supernatural.

I encourage you to take a moment to reflect back on your life so far. Can you point to any divine invasions you may have experienced?

- Can you look back and see a supernatural answer to prayer—when you prayed for something and only God could be the one who answered that prayer?
- Can you look back and see a word of encouragement that you needed that came at just the right time?

- Can you remember a need you had that no one or few people knew about that was dramatically met, and there's no other way to explain it except the hand of God?
- Can you recall something that happened in your life at just the right time—an event that only God could have orchestrated to happen when it did?

It's my hope that this book will assure you that God is at work in the world today and encourage you to ask God to work in your life as well. Perhaps you will recall times when the Lord intervened in your life or the life of someone important to you, and you'll pause to give Him praise.

However, I realize that you've also had times when you desperately needed a miracle and one didn't come. Maybe you need a miracle right now. And when you hear stories about other believers who experience God's divine invasions, such as the miraculous protection of my family members on the road that rainy afternoon, you wonder, *Why isn't God giving me a miracle?*

If that sounds like you right now, then let me assure you: *God is still in the miracle-working business.* That's why God preserved so many stories of miracles in the Bible, along with stories of modern-day miracles such as those you'll read in this book: to teach you that He is able to answer your prayers and intervene in your life. Yes, God is able to supernaturally work a miracle in your life, if He chooses to do so. But even if He chooses not to, as we're going to see, He still is able to unleash His supernatural power in giving you peace so that you can endure the circumstances you're experiencing.

What Is a Miracle?

As we begin our study of miracles, it's important to clarify exactly what we're talking about when we refer to a "miracle." As you've likely discovered, a word that means one thing to you can mean something entirely different to someone else.

Today, the word *miracle* is used in ways that have nothing to do with God. We talk about the "Miracle on Ice," when the United States hockey team defeated the Soviet Union at the 1980 Olympics, and watch the Christmas movie *Miracle on 34th Street*. In pharmacies and grocery stores, we find dozens of "miracle" drugs and "miracle" beauty products. And I haven't even touched on Miracle Whip, Miracle-Gro, Miracle-Ear, Miracle Wipes, or an event that at least comes close to an actual miracle, the "Miracle on the Hudson," which I wrote about in my book *Courageous*.[2]

We also hear the word *miracle* thrown around lightly in reference to God. Do you know somebody who is always going around talking about their miracles? For some people, it seems every day they have a miracle from God. They say things like, "I had a miracle today: I got a parking space up front when it was raining!" Or "I got the very last sale item before the store sold out—it's a miracle!"

With all the different ways *miracle* is used today, it's no wonder we get confused as to its real meaning. We don't want to call something a miracle too loosely, but we also don't want to define it so narrowly that nothing could possibly be considered a miracle today. When we're talking about the supernatural activities of our miracle-working God, what do we mean? When it comes to defining what a miracle is or isn't, we must consult the Bible.

In the New Testament, we see four Greek words that describe what a miracle is. Let's look at each of these words, and then I'll show you a fifth phrase that refers to God's miraculous interventions in people's lives throughout Scripture.

Mighty Works

In the New Testament, the Greek word *dunamis* is translated as "mighty works," "great miracles," or "extraordinary miracles." We get our words *dynamite* and *dynamic* from it. *Dunamis* literally means "power" and refers to supernatural works that cannot be duplicated by natural agents.

Two passages in the book of Acts demonstrate the explosive nature of this word. First of all, in Acts 8, we are introduced to a magician named Simon, whose demonically empowered sorcery astonished the people of Samaria (vv. 9–11). Some of you have been to places in the world where demonic activity has a free hand, and you may have experienced similar astonishment upon seeing dark magic. Witch doctors and sorcerers are usually celebrities in their communities, as Simon was in Samaria. They called him "the Great Power of God" (v. 10) and thought he was the biggest thing ever to hit town.

That is, until the evangelist Philip came along, "preaching the good news about the kingdom of God and the name of Jesus Christ" (v. 12). To authenticate Philip's message, God performed "signs and great miracles"—*dunamis*—through Philip (v. 13). These great miracles so impressed Simon that he "believed," was "baptized," and was "constantly amazed" at the "signs and great miracles taking place" (v. 13). Today, we might say Simon's head exploded at the dynamic power of God.

The other passage that uses *dunamis* in reference to miracles is Acts 19. Paul was ministering in the spiritually dark and depraved city of Ephesus. Because the Temple of Artemis—one of the Seven Wonders of the Ancient World—was located there, Ephesus attracted all sorts of eccentric characters practicing pagan magic, sorcery, and incantations. As a result, satanic activity was widespread in the city. The closest equivalent I can think of in America is Salem, Massachusetts. It's a pretty town with a beautiful harbor, but because of its history with the Salem witch trials in 1692–93, it's filled with shops devoted to witches and the occult.

In Ephesus, the Lord used the apostle Paul to throw a hand grenade into the middle of all that demonic power. Acts 19:11 says, "God was performing extraordinary miracles by the hands of Paul."

The city of Ephesus was so steeped in paganism and idolatry that the Lord used extraordinary means to break Satan's hold on the people there. One of those means was the use of Paul's "handkerchiefs or aprons," which were miraculously imbued with God's power. According to verse 12, these items were "carried from his body to the sick, and the diseases left them and the evil spirits went out." The Greek word translated as "handkerchief" literally means "sweat cloths," like a sweatband, and the word for "apron" refers to a workman's apron, like the one Paul would have worn while doing leatherwork. Paul may have been practicing his trade as a tentmaker while in Ephesus, since these items were used by the Lord to perform miracles.

Misusing this verse, some Christian charlatans today claim that the power of God transfers from them into their own handkerchiefs—which can be yours . . . for a price. All you need to do is send in a donation, the bigger the better, and the preacher will send you a handkerchief used to wipe the sweat from his forehead. And the promise? As soon as you touch that handkerchief, you'll get health for your body and wealth for your bank account. Nonsense! Don't be duped by such schemes. (In chapter 7, I'll show you specific ways to avoid being deceived by counterfeit miracles.) Though God can and does still do mighty works today, false teachers play on your emotions for the purpose of robbing you of your money. Their promises are propaganda, and their handkerchiefs are only as valuable as the stuff you blow into them. Remember, the way we recognize a true teacher today is not by mighty works but by fidelity to Scripture.

Signs

The Greek word *semeion* is almost always translated as "signs," signifying supernatural works that show something about the worker of these signs. They are divine fingerprints. For example, when prophets or apostles performed signs in the Bible, those miracles pointed to their authority as authentic spokespeople for God. Paul made this clear when he wrote, "The signs of a true apostle were performed among you with all perseverance, by signs and wonders and miracles" (2 Cor. 12:12). What Paul meant by "signs" was literally "attesting miracles"—miracles that proved his authenticity as God's apostle.

The same kinds of attesting miracles also apply to Jesus. Isaiah 11 and 35 anticipate the coming Messiah as a miracle worker who would perform signs to prove His divinity, such as giving sight to the blind and enabling the lame to walk. And that's exactly what we see in the ministry of Jesus. In his Gospel, the apostle John included seven "signs" performed by Jesus Christ, each one pointing to something significant about our Lord.[3]

I believe God still uses signs to confirm His existence and reveal Himself to people today. In fact, don't be surprised if God brings you to a point in your life when the only thing you know to do is to pray—and then He will send some kind of sign to encourage you that He's still at work in your life.

But, as I mentioned earlier, I don't believe God needs or uses people to perform signs anymore. If you encounter or see on television someone who claims to perform signs, such as having the gift of healing apart from medical means, the question to ask is, Who receives the glory: Christ or the faith healer? When God uses signs today, He does it directly, and the purpose is to point to Himself.

Wonders

The third Greek word used for miracles is *teras*, translated as "wonders." *Teras* refers to supernatural works that cause or evoke astonishment, amazement, or awe in those witnessing the miracle. Have you ever seen something that just took your breath away? You stood there and said, "I can't believe it!" That's what a wonder is.

Used sixteen times in the New Testament, *teras* ("wonders") often appears side by side with *semeion* ("signs"). The word *wonders* emphasizes the reaction of people to miracles. For example, when Peter delivered his sermon in Acts 2, he said, "Men of Israel, listen to these words: Jesus the Nazarene, a man attested to you by God with miracles and *wonders* and *signs* which God performed through Him in your midst, just as you yourselves know" (v. 22). The message of salvation preached by Peter and the other apostles was "first spoken through the Lord" and "confirmed . . . by those who heard" the message (Heb. 2:3). It was also confirmed by God through "*signs* and *wonders* and by various miracles and by gifts of the Holy Spirit according to His own will" (v. 4).

God's miraculous wonders are all around us, if we'll only take the time to pay attention to them.

The reaction of the disciples to the miraculous sign of Jesus's resurrection was similar: wonder and worship. Peter and John stood in amazement at the empty tomb with the graveclothes intact (John 20:3–8), Mary Magdalene clung to Jesus (vv. 16–17), the disciples rejoiced with "amazement" (vv. 19–20; Luke 24:41), and Thomas worshiped (John 20:27–28). This is our response to God's wonders.

Have you stood in wonder at God's creation? Have you been awestruck by a sunrise or sunset, by the majesty of the mountains, or by the power of the sea? God's miraculous wonders are all around us, if we'll only take the time to pay attention to them.

Works

Fourth, the New Testament describes some miracles with the Greek word *erga*, translated as "works." In certain contexts, this word refers to supernatural works that cannot be performed by anyone other than Jesus Christ. These "works" go beyond any human efforts and are unique to Jesus as the Messiah.

When John the Baptist was thrown into prison, he wrestled with doubts about whether his cousin, Jesus, was the Messiah. So John sent his disciples to Jesus, asking, "Are You the Expected One, or shall we look for someone else?" (Matt. 11:3). Jesus said, "Go and report to John what you hear and see" (v. 4). Jesus then listed five works only the Messiah could perform: "the blind receive sight and the lame walk, the lepers are cleansed and the deaf hear, the dead are raised up," and on top of that, "the poor have the gospel preached to them" (v. 5).[4]

These are the very works Jesus challenged the religious leaders with when they wanted to stone Him for claiming to be the "Son of God" (John 10:36). He said to them, "If I do not do the works of My Father, do not believe Me; but if I do them [the works of the Father], though you do not believe Me, believe the *works*, so that you may know and understand that the Father is in Me, and I in the Father"

(vv. 37–38). In other words, "so you may know and understand that I am the Son of God."

Miraculous Providence

Finally, the Bible also includes acts of God's *miraculous providence* in the lives of His children. These types of divine invasions, often accomplished within the framework of natural laws, demonstrate the hand of God in orchestrating His plan for our lives.

Providence is one of those words we use but don't really understand what it means. The word *providence* comes from two words: *pro*, which means "before," and *video*, which means "to see." Providence refers to God's ability to see beforehand what happens to us.

Did you know your situation today, whatever it is, didn't take God by surprise? There's nothing that happens to you that takes God by surprise. That illness. That termination. That divorce. As much of a shock as it was to you, it was no shock to God. He sees it all.

Providence refers to the fact that God is in control of every detail of His creation, which means He's in control of your life and my life.

Here's the comforting truth: God not only sees our lives beforehand but also plans our lives beforehand. *Providence* refers to the fact that God is in control of every detail of His creation, which means He's in control of your life and my life.

We see God's miraculous providence throughout Scripture:

- In Genesis 37–50, we see *God's miraculous providence in the life of Joseph*. Betrayed by his brothers and sold into slavery, Joseph was raised up by the providence of God to become the head of Potiphar's household. While there, Joseph was falsely accused of rape and thrown into prison, where God's hand of providence lifted him up to be the second in command to Pharaoh, saving Israel from a great famine.
- In Exodus 2, we see *God's miraculous providence in the life of Moses*. When Pharaoh ordered every Hebrew male baby to be killed, Moses's parents covered a wicker basket in tar, put baby Moses in it, and floated him in the Nile River. Through God's miraculous providence, Pharaoh's daughter came out to the Nile to bathe, saw baby Moses, and decided to take him to be her own—and Moses's own mother, Jochebed, ended up in Pharaoh's household nursing Moses and helping him to grow into the man God would use to deliver Israel out of Egyptian bondage.
- In Acts 16, we see *God's miraculous providence in the early church*. Paul and Silas were imprisoned in Philippi when an earthquake struck, and all the prisoners' chains were "unfastened" (v. 26). Notably, the shackles didn't simply become unbolted

> from a weakened wall. Rather, through God's miraculous providence, the clasps that held the shackles shut were suddenly unlocked, setting Paul and Silas free.

Over and over throughout Scripture, as well as in our lives today, we see God's supernatural care for His children. Through His miraculous providence, God guides us through an impression on our hearts while in prayer or "a word spoken in right circumstances" by a friend (Prov. 25:11). Miracles of providence come through modern medical procedures that save lives and help us recover from disease. His divine invasions cause us to run late and avoid a terrible accident that occurred five minutes before.

Most of the stories you'll encounter in this book—as well as most of the divine invasions in your life today—fall under this category: the miraculous providence of God.

Why Does God Perform Miracles?

When God acts, He doesn't act capriciously. Nothing God does is impulsive. Everything He does has a purpose, including working miracles. There are at least five purposes for miracles.

To Glorify God and Christ

The glory of God is a major theme running throughout the Bible. The Greek word translated as "glorify" (*doksazo*) means to magnify or enlarge. To *glorify* God is to enlarge Him in the minds of other people.

When Jesus healed a bedridden paralytic, the man "went home glorifying God," and those who witnessed the miracle "began glorifying God" (Luke 5:26). When Jesus raised a widow's son from the dead, the witnesses were overcome by awe and "began glorifying God, saying, 'A great prophet has arisen among us!' and, 'God has visited His people!'" (7:16). And when Jesus healed a blind man, he "began . . . glorifying God; and when all the people saw it, they gave praise to God" (18:43).

One reason God created us is to be human magnifying glasses who enlarge God in the minds of other people. When people see God's miraculous works in our lives, they see how powerful, loving, and wise God truly is.

To Demonstrate God's Sovereignty

God's *sovereignty* refers to His complete control over all of His creation. Every now and then, we all need a reminder of God's absolute authority over His creation, and miracles are the way He provides those reminders.

Before the Lord unleashed the ten plagues on Egypt, He told Moses the reason for these divine judgments was to "bring out . . . My people the sons of Israel, from the land of Egypt" (Exod. 7:4). But that wasn't the only reason. God also said, "The Egyptians *shall know that I am the* L*ORD*, when I stretch out My hand on Egypt and bring out the sons of Israel from their midst" (v. 5).

The forty-year wilderness sojourn also demonstrated God's sovereignty. This is what He told that second generation of Israelites: "I have led you forty years in the wilderness; your clothes have not worn out on you, and your sandal has not worn out on your foot . . . in order that you *might know that I am the LORD your God*" (Deut. 29:5–6).

To Authenticate God's Messengers

When Nicodemus had his nighttime interview with Christ, he said, "Rabbi, we know that You have come from God as a teacher; for *no one can do these signs that You do unless God is with him*" (John 3:2). During Peter's sermon on Pentecost, he said, "Men of Israel, listen to these words: Jesus the Nazarene, *a man attested to you by God with miracles and wonders and signs* which God performed through Him in your midst, just as you yourselves know" (Acts 2:22).

A word of caution here: Though God used miracles to authenticate His prophets and apostles in Scripture, the way we judge whether a messenger is from God today is not by his or her ability to perform signs and wonders; it's by his or her faithfulness to the Word of God. Many people have been deceived into believing that certain faith healers and televangelists are the real deal, only to discover they've been supporting frauds and phonies.

Think about Pharaoh's magicians, for example. They had the ability to counterfeit the miracles of Moses. Just because a miraculous event takes place does not mean God is necessarily behind that person's action. Do not be deceived by so-called miracles. Satan has the ability to perform counterfeit miracles. (I'll talk more about this in chapter 7.) We must test every experience, every truth, not by whether it is miraculous but by whether it aligns with the Word of God.

To Confirm God's Message

Along with authenticating God's messengers, miracles also confirm God's message. When Paul and Barnabas visited the city of Iconium, many people came to faith in Christ. Luke said Paul and Barnabas "spent a long time there speaking boldly with reliance upon the Lord, who was testifying to the word of His grace, *granting that signs and wonders be done by their hands*" (Acts 14:3). The salvation the people of Iconium received was first "spoken through the Lord" and "was confirmed to us by those who heard, God also testifying with them, *both by signs and wonders and by various miracles and by gifts of the Holy Spirit according to His own will*" (Heb. 2:3–4).

I remember a time when God's miraculous providence confirmed His message in my life. One evening, while I was a student at Baylor University, I received an unmistakable impression from the Lord that I would one day be the pastor of First Baptist Church in Dallas. I kept what I believed was a promise from the Lord to myself for years, not even sharing it with my wife.

When the pastoral search committee from First Dallas spoke with me about coming to serve as their pastor, I kept mum. I didn't tell anyone because I wanted to ensure that if the call came to serve as the pastor at First Baptist Dallas, it would come about because of God's supernatural confirmation, not as a result of my manipulation. When the church unanimously called me as pastor, in 2007, I then told the committee and congregation that God had impressed this on me many years before.

Sometimes God gives supernatural signs to lead us, while other times He gives supernatural signs to confirm that we are making the right decision. We must be open and attentive to His leading, understanding that God works His miracles for a purpose.

To Encourage Greater Faith

Comedian Woody Allen once said, "If only God would give me some sign. If He would just speak to me once. Anything. One sentence. Two words. If He would just cough."[5] People say if they could see a miracle, then they would believe in God—but signs don't necessarily cause people to believe.

However, miracles can be the impetus to greater faith. We see this in the lives of many Israelites who witnessed the ten plagues. Exodus 14:31 says, "When Israel saw the great power which the LORD had used against the Egyptians, the people feared the LORD, and they believed in the LORD and in His servant Moses."

The apostle John couldn't have been clearer in linking Jesus's miracles to saving faith when he wrote, "Many other signs Jesus also performed in the presence of the disciples, which are not written in this book; but these have been written so that you may believe that Jesus is the Christ, the Son of God; and that believing you may have life in His name" (John 20:30–31).

Do you have a story of a miracle that either prompted you to believe in Christ or strengthened your faith in Christ? If so, tell your story to someone. You never know, it might place that person on the path to salvation or encourage someone's lagging faith.

An Overview of *Divine Invasions*

In the chapters that follow, we will see that God is still divinely invading our lives today through miracles of power, protection, provision, and healing. In chapters 2 through 5, we will look at each of these kinds of miracles. Then, in chapter 6, we'll turn to the difficult question of what to do when your miracle doesn't come. I'll address this reality as comprehensively and compassionately as I can, not only offering biblical answers but also providing encouragement to remain faithful to the Lord. Finally, in chapter 7, I'll share some practical guidance that will help you learn how to discern authentic miracles.

As we begin our study of miracles together, let me give you a word of caution: Don't become so enamored with the stories told in this book that you miss the Storyteller—the one behind the stories. The miracles mentioned in this book might be compelling, but I urge you not to get so caught up in the stories of the supernatural that you miss the point.

Keep in mind that these stories of miracles are intended to strengthen your faith in our miracle-working God. It's my prayer that when you've finished this book, you'll recognize God's divine invasions in your own life and boldly call on Him whenever you need Him to act.

CHAPTER 2

MIRACLES OF POWER

WHEN I WAS A SENIOR at Baylor University in Waco, Texas, I had a divinely orchestrated encounter that changed my life.

Three years earlier, I had arrived at college filled with anticipation, eager to dive deep into the study of the Scriptures. While I was in high school, I'd had the overwhelming sense that God was calling me to be a pastor, and I obeyed this calling by getting involved in ministry-related activities such as sharing the gospel with other students and leading Bible studies. After high school graduation, I was eager to go to Baylor, a Baptist university, to study the Bible and prepare for pastoral ministry—but my college experience turned out to be vastly different from what I expected. I didn't realize that, at the time, many professors at Baylor didn't believe in the inerrancy of the Bible.

Year after year, as I attended classes taught by professors who claimed the Bible was filled with contradictions, errors, and inconsistencies, I began to doubt God's Word and His calling me to pastoral ministry. How could I commit my life to preaching a book that was apparently filled with myths and mistakes? I seriously considered abandoning my calling, changing career goals, and perhaps turning my back on Christianity altogether.

Then the Lord graciously steered into my path some key people who believed in the inerrancy of the Bible for sound intellectual reasons. They convinced me I didn't have to commit intellectual suicide to trust in God's Word. They also encouraged me to attend the Urbana Missions Conference in Champaign, Illinois, during Christmas break.

On the final night of the conference, I sat in the top row of a huge basketball arena filled with thousands of university students. I was still wrestling with whether the Bible was really the Word of God and whether I should go into ministry when the evangelist Billy Graham walked onto the stage.

During his message that evening, Billy shared that he, too, had a crisis of faith while he was a student at a Bible college. One night, Billy took a walk along a trail at the Forest Home Conference Center in California. About fifty yards from the main path was a large rock he sat on for a long time, crying out to the Lord with his Bible spread open on a tree stump. Finally, with a spirit of surrender, he prayed, "O God! There are many things in this book I do not understand. There are many problems with it for which I have no solution. . . . Father, I am going to accept this as Thy Word—by faith! I'm going to allow faith to go beyond my intellectual questions and doubts, and I will believe this to be Your inspired Word."[1]

Today at the Forest Home Conference Center, there is a bronze tablet by that rock identifying it as the "Stone of Witness" where Billy Graham accepted once and for all the absolute authority of Scripture. The Lord heard his prayer, and Dr. Graham fulfilled his promise to preach the Bible faithfully as God's inerrant Word.

As I listened to that story with tears streaming down my face, Dr. Graham's prayer became my prayer—and the Lord, in His grace, answered it for me as well. I realized God had directed me to that conference to hear Billy Graham's story of spiritual struggle—the same struggle I had been wrestling with. But then the Lord added a "cherry" to the "spiritual sundae" He served me that night!

After Dr. Graham finished his presentation and the evening's conference session concluded, I somehow missed the exit and ended up in a freight elevator with him and his evangelistic team. I said to him, "Dr. Graham, you'll never know what your message meant to me tonight." I told him about my struggle with doubt and shared the commitment I'd made that night in response to his story. He congratulated me and wrote an encouraging note in my spiral notebook that I will treasure forever.

Whenever I'm tempted to doubt God's Word, I think back to that evening and look at Billy Graham's message in my notebook—yes, I still have it—and am reminded of that cold night in December 1976, when God divinely intervened in my life to confirm the reliability of His Word and His calling for me.

If you're a follower of Christ, I imagine that you, too, have a story like this. Somewhere in your past, you experienced a divine invasion when God demonstrated His care for you in some way. The particulars of your story will differ from mine, but the Lord's grace and provision are the same, just as the Scripture teaches: "Jesus Christ is the same yesterday and today and forever" (Heb. 13:8).

God's Power on Display in Five Periods

Most Christians would be quick to agree that God's power is as potent today as it was during the days of Scripture. But let's face it, sometimes it feels like His power is lacking when we need it most.

This reminds me of an experience I had during the first cruise I hosted with *Pathway to Victory*. As I stood on the deck and gazed out over the ocean, seeing only water around me for miles and miles, I was overwhelmed by an awareness of how puny and small I was in comparison to God's endless vastness. I could relate to the words of the old French fishermen's prayer: "My God, protect me, my boat is so small, and Your sea is so big."[2]

Although you and I are created in the image of God, we're weak and small compared to many forces in this fallen world. We need God's power to strengthen us and defend us. Like David, we pray, "Bend down, O Lord, and hear my prayer; answer me, for I need help. Protect me, for I am devoted to you. Save me, for I serve you and trust you. You are my God" (Ps. 86:1–2 NLT).

As I mentioned in chapter 1, most of our experiences of God's power in our lives today fall under the category of His *miraculous providence*—subtle demonstrations of His care for us. He supernaturally invades our lives by orchestrating various events and people to work out His plan for us, like the experience I had at the missions conference.

Although every miracle involves God's power, there are certain miracles that display His supernatural power in a dramatic way. When we investigate the pages of Scripture, we discover five periods of time with God's power on full display in dramatic ways. Four of those periods are past, and one is future. Like grapes on a vine, these dramatic demonstrations of God's miraculous power are clustered around certain individuals during times when the Lord was doing (and will do) something unique.[3] Let's take a look at each of these five periods of God's miraculous power.

Moses and Joshua

Israel's exodus from Egyptian bondage signaled that God was in the process of doing something brand-new: taking a single family line—that of Abraham, Isaac, and Jacob—and forging it into a nation. The first cluster of dramatic demonstrations of God's power began with the miracle of the burning bush, when God appeared to Moses and called him to lead the Israelites out of Egypt (Exod. 3:1–22). From there, dramatic demonstrations of God's power multiplied:

- Aaron's staff turned into a snake and ate the magicians' snakes and staffs (7:9–12).
- Ten plagues ravaged Egypt (7:15–11:8).
- The Red Sea parted, and the Israelites passed through on dry ground (14:21–31).
- God provided manna from heaven and quail for food (16:1–35).
- Water flowed from a rock (17:1–7).
- The Ten Commandments were written by the finger of God (20:1–17).

On into the books of Leviticus, Numbers, and Deuteronomy, God's miracles of power confirmed His presence with the Israelites.

This first cluster of miracles continues into the book of Joshua. When Moses died, Joshua led the nation into the land promised to them by God. They crossed the Jordan River at flood stage on dry land (Josh. 3:7–17), Joshua encountered the preincarnate Christ—the "commander of the LORD's army" (5:13–15 NLT)—the walls collapsed and allowed them to conquer Jericho (6:15–21), and Joshua called on the sun to stand still (10:12–14).

Elijah and Elisha

By the time the nation of Israel was well established and living in peace and prosperity under David's and Solomon's rules, God's miracles of power trailed off. But when the nation divided into two, and the northern kingdom of Israel fell into idolatry and corruption, the Lord had a new message: one of divine judgment. His chosen messenger was a man from Tishbe named Elijah.

Similar to the miracle of the burning bush, the first miracle of power God demonstrated in the life of Elijah occurred in the wilderness: a divine meal supplied by ravens after Elijah predicted a drought (1 Kings 17:1–6). When the creek Elijah used for water dried up, the Lord sent him to a Gentile widow, where he stocked her dwindling pantry and raised her son from the dead (vv. 8–23). Later, Elijah challenged the corrupt king, Ahab, and his idolatrous priests to a showdown on Mount Carmel, where the Lord breathed fire from heaven (18:17–40), followed by heavy rains (vv. 41–45). God performed other miracles through Elijah, culminating in the whirlwind of the fiery chariot that transported the prophet alive to heaven (2 Kings 2:11–12).

God hadn't finished judging Israel when Elijah was swooped up to heaven. His protégé, Elisha, was left behind to continue as God's representative. Elisha repeated many of the same miracles as Elijah but overall performed almost twice as many, including predicting pregnancy for a barren woman (4:14–17) then raising her son to life when he died (vv. 29–37). Elisha also cured the leper Naaman (5:1, 9–14) while cursing Gehazi with leprosy (vv. 20–27), and he performed many other miracles during his lifetime.

Daniel and His Friends

Because Israel persisted in worshiping other gods and refused to learn the lessons of the miracles performed through His messengers Elijah and Elisha, God handed the Israelites over to the Assyrians in 722 BC. One hundred and seventeen years later, in 605 BC, the southern kingdom of Judah became the puppet-state of the Babylonians, who carted off some of the leading citizens of Jerusalem, including Daniel and his three friends Hananiah (Shadrach), Mishael (Meshach), and Azariah (Abed-nego).

If you've spent any time in Sunday school, you're likely familiar with some of the miracles that took place during Judah's exile in Babylon and were recorded in the book of Daniel. Refusing to eat food sacrificed to idols, Daniel and his friends chose a diet of vegetables and water. The Lord honored their commitment by giving them strong bodies and robust minds on this diet (1:8–17). Daniel was given the insight to know what Nebuchadnezzar dreamed and the ability to interpret the dream when the king's wise men couldn't (2:1–47). For their obedience to worship God alone, Shadrach, Meshach, and Abed-nego were thrown into the fiery furnace. And yet, the preincarnate Christ was with them, protecting them from the flames and the heat (3:1–30).

Again, Daniel was granted the power to recount one of the king's dreams and to interpret it. This time, Daniel warned Nebuchadnezzar to submit to God's grace or face God's wrath, which would come in the form of madness (4:1–33). And then there was, of course, Daniel's ability to read God's mysterious message left on the wall of Belshazzar's banquet hall (5:1–30) and Daniel's quiet night in the lions' den (6:1–23).

These demonstrations of God's power all occurred within about a seventy-year timeframe during which the Israelites—uprooted from their homeland—needed dramatic and consistent reminders of God's faithfulness and power.

Jesus and the Apostles

When we turn the page from the Old Testament to the New Testament, we see God doing the most dramatic work of all: the incarnation of His Son, Jesus, along with Christ's death and resurrection. In support of His claim that He is the Son of God, the long-awaited Messiah, Jesus worked miracles up and down the length of Israel, especially early in His ministry.

According to the Gospels, Jesus performed thirty-seven miracles during His earthly ministry. Some are unique to Matthew—healing two blind men (9:27–31) and finding money in a fish's mouth (17:24–27); some are unique to Mark—healing a deaf man (7:31–37) and a blind man at Bethsaida (8:22–26); some are unique to Luke—raising a widow's son (7:11–17) and healing a woman who had suffered for eighteen years (13:10–17); and some are unique to John—turning water into wine (2:1–11) and raising Lazarus from the dead (11:1–44). Interestingly, there's only one miracle that is recorded in all four Gospels: the feeding of the five thousand (Matt. 14:13–21; Mark 6:32–44; Luke 9:10–17; John 6:1–14).

According to the Gospels, Jesus performed thirty-seven miracles during His earthly ministry.

Following the death, resurrection, and ascension of Jesus Christ, the Holy Spirit came to indwell all believers permanently, and the church was born in Jerusalem. The leaders of the church—the apostles—were empowered by the Holy Spirit and followed in Jesus's footsteps as miracle workers. They healed the lame and paralyzed (Acts 3:6; 9:34; 14:10), cast out demons (16:18), and brought the dead back to life (9:40; 20:10).[4]

Right about now you might be getting misty-eyed about the "good old days," thinking to yourself, *Man, it would have been great to live during the time of Moses or Elijah or Daniel or the early days of the church to witness the stunning power of God.* Would it surprise you if I told you that it wouldn't have been so great? Those were times of significant societal and political upheaval. Would you really want to wander the desert for forty years, eating nothing but manna and quail? Or would you want to live in a country where political corruption and tyranny ruled, drought and disease were a constant reality, and idolatry and immorality ran rampant, even worse than today? That's what was taking place during the time of Elijah and Elisha. And would you really like to be carted off, against your will, to a foreign country as Daniel and his friends were?

Okay, I get your point, you're probably thinking. But I can hear you asking, "What about living when Jesus walked the earth? Wouldn't you want to be one of the first Christians in Jerusalem?" No. I might have been one of the people who sang hosannas to Christ at the beginning of the week and shouted "Crucify Him!" at the end of the week. And you might have too. Plus, would you really want to be part of a church where you could suddenly be struck dead for lying to the Holy Spirit, like Ananias and Sapphira?

We should be grateful for the era in which God has chosen for us to live.

We should be grateful for the era in which God has chosen for us to live. Although we may face a culture that is increasingly ungodly and live under a government that is increasingly dysfunctional, compared to other ages of human history this is a time of relative political and societal calm. And think of the unique spiritual blessings we can experience that no believer in the past was able to enjoy: We have the complete Word of God at our fingertips, something none of the people who lived during the days of the Old or New Testaments had. We have the indwelling Holy Spirit, which wasn't true of believers during the days of Moses, Joshua, Elijah, Elisha, Daniel and his friends, or even Jesus's incarnation. I suggest we make this Jewish prayer our own prayer: "Privileged, O Lord, are we to live in this generation."[5]

I told you there are five periods when miracles clustered together. So far, we've seen four of them, which happened in the past. The fifth, which is yet to come, is a time no one wants to live through.

Satan and God

Paul made clear in 2 Thessalonians, as John did in the book of Revelation, that the fifth and final cluster of miracles of power will occur during the end times—the seven years of tribulation that will start with the rapture of the church and end with the second coming of Christ. This is certainly a unique period in human history, unlike any period before it, and it doesn't follow the pattern of other miraculous eras. Instead of God working through His faithful servants or His Son, many of the miracles in this era will be performed by Satan and his Antichrist.

Paul warned of the appearance of a "lawless one . . . whose coming is in accord with the activity of Satan, with all power and signs and false wonders" (2 Thess. 2:8–9). This "lawless one"—the Antichrist—will perform many so-called miracles to validate Satan's false claim that the

Antichrist is the savior of the world and that the people of the world should worship him. Satan's "lying wonders" (v. 9 KJV) are scattered throughout the book of Revelation. God brings a series of devastating miraculous judgments upon the unrepentant who follow Satan and the Antichrist rather than turning in faith to follow God and Christ.

The book of Revelation culminates in the great miracle of the new heavens and the new earth where "there will no longer be any curse" or all the baggage that came because of it (Rev. 22:3). That's the miracle we're all looking forward to.

God's Power Promised for Today

Just because God's dramatic powers were (and will be) displayed during these five clusters of time doesn't mean His power is diminished in any way today. Far from it. *Nothing* of or in our God is limited. That's why we say God is *omnipotent*. That's a ten-cent theological term that means "all-powerful."[6] God can do anything that is in accordance with His will, including working a miracle in your life. His power is available for us today because He has promised to make it available.[7]

Isaiah 40:28 says, "Do you not know? Have you not heard? The Everlasting God, the LORD, the Creator of the ends of the earth does not become weary or tired. His understanding is inscrutable." Notice how God described Himself: as "everlasting," not bound by time; as "the Creator of the ends of the earth," not restricted to one parcel of land; as the tireless Lord, not run-down and old; and as the inscrutable God, not a children's book deity who is easily understood.

Have you forgotten these eternal truths? It's easy to do, especially when life comes crashing down on your head. But don't! This is your God. Pause for a moment and think about that. Let it settle deep into your soul. This God is the source of your power in your time of need. I like how Christian philosopher Peter Kreeft described God's power: "God has more power in one breath of his spirit than all the winds of war, all the nuclear bombs, all the energy of all the suns in all the galaxies, all the fury of Hell itself."[8]

God can do anything that is in accordance with His will, including working a miracle in your life.

Now, some of you may be thinking, *Pastor, I did as you suggested. I thought deeply about how great God is, and I can't shake the feeling that He's too great to care for me and my puny problems.* I can't answer that any better than Bible scholar Thomas Constable did: "God is not too great to care. He is too great not to care."[9] And that's what we see in the closing verses of Isaiah 40:

> He gives strength to the weary,
> And to him who lacks might He increases power.
> Though youths grow weary and tired,
> And vigorous young men stumble badly,
> Yet those who wait for the Lord
> Will gain new strength;

> They will mount up with wings like eagles,
> They will run and not get tired,
> They will walk and not become weary. (vv. 29–31)

God doesn't just possess all power; He gives power to the weak. God doesn't just possess all energy; He gives energy to the fatigued. All you need do is "wait for the LORD"—rest in hope, looking to God to supply your need—and He will give you strength, exchanging His power for your powerlessness.

Once a man approached Jesus, asking the Lord to deliver his son from a demonic spirit that threatened to harm the boy. The father said to Jesus, "If You can do anything, take pity on us and help us!" (Mark 9:22). Jesus answered, "'If You can'?" (v. 23). The troubled father wanted to know whether Jesus had power over demonic forces. But Jesus wanted to know whether the father had faith in God's all-consuming power because He said to him, "All things are possible to him who believes" in the all-powerful God (v. 23). The Scripture is clear on this point. In fact, it's repeated throughout the Old and New Testaments: *Nothing is impossible with God*. We just need to come to the omnipotent God in faith.[10] If you don't remember anything else from this chapter, remember this: The same power of God on dramatic display during these five times in history is working in your life right now.

The Principles for Experiencing God's Power

Scripture lays out four principles we need to understand if we want to access God's power in our lives. If we think about these principles as classes in a college degree program, the first would be considered a prerequisite, while principles two to four would be considered classes for a major.

Principle #1: God's Power Is Primarily for His Children

In the Sermon on the Mount, Jesus mentioned a truth that theologians call *common grace*. It refers to what is universally true—for all times and all people—no matter one's relationship with God. Jesus put it in terms everyone can understand: "[God] causes His sun to rise on the evil and the good, and sends rain on the righteous and the unrighteous" (Matt. 5:45).

While God shows His goodness by blessing all people with sunshine and rain, He generally reserves the unleashing of His miraculous power only for those who are truly His children. This doesn't mean God is unconcerned for others. He certainly is concerned for all people, including unbelievers. If He wasn't, then He wouldn't have sent His Son as a sacrifice for their sin. But it does mean God's children hold a special place in His heart. The apostle John described God's special love for His children this way: "See *how great a love the Father has bestowed on us*, that we would be called children of God; and such we are" (1 John 3:1).

God's special care for His children is not only biblical, but it also makes sense. After all, every parent's primary concern is for the welfare of his or her own child, even if we don't want to see other children harmed or deprived of the necessities of life. For example, when my girls played team sports and had a physical run-in with either a teammate or a member of the opposing team, I didn't want the other player to be injured, but my main concern was for the health and safety of my own child.

What this means to you can be boiled down to one simple question: *Are you a child of God?* Your answer to this question is the prerequisite for experiencing the power of God in your life. If you want to know God's power, then you must respond in faith to the power of His gospel—the good news of Jesus's death and resurrection. Paul wrote in Romans 1:16, "For I am not ashamed of the gospel, for it is the power of God for salvation to everyone who believes." (For more on how to become a Christian, see the conclusion, "Your Divine Invitation.")

When Jesus came to earth and began His ministry, He was anointed "with the Holy Spirit and with power" (Acts 10:38). His death on the cross, as Paul said, "is the power of God" unto salvation (1 Cor. 1:18). And His resurrection displayed God's power over death (Eph. 1:19–20). God's power continues to be displayed in Christ's ability to save those who believe and to keep them saved (1 Cor. 6:14; 1 Pet. 1:5). So the question remains: *Are you a child of God?*

Principle #2: God's Power Is Generated by the Holy Spirit

Once you trust in Christ for the forgiveness of your sins, you become a child of God. The apostle John wrote, "As many as received [Jesus], to them He gave the right to become children of God, even to those who believe in His name" (John 1:12). With your adoption into God's family, the Lord gives you a wonderful gift: the Holy Spirit. We'll look at the work of the Spirit in your life in the next chapter. For now, I want to focus on two aspects of the Spirit related to God's power in your life.

First, your expression of saving faith in Jesus corresponds immediately with the Spirit taking up residence in your life. Theologians call this *the indwelling of the Spirit*. Paul made it clear in Romans 8:9 that every genuine believer is in the Spirit, and the Spirit is in them. Speaking to Christians, Paul said, "You are not in the flesh but in the Spirit, if indeed the Spirit of God dwells in you. But if anyone does not have the Spirit of Christ, he does not belong to Him."

Just because you have the permanent indwelling of the Holy Spirit doesn't mean you are yielding your life to the Holy Spirit's control. This is the second aspect I want to focus on, what theologians call *the filling of the Spirit*. Paul commanded all believers, "Do not get drunk with wine, for that is dissipation, but be filled with the Spirit" (Eph. 5:18). Paul means you shouldn't be controlled by your selfish, sinful self—living for your pleasures. That's what's behind the idea of drunkenness, which Roman philosopher Seneca said was "nothing but voluntary insanity."[11] Paul's point isn't strictly about overdrinking but refers to any activity that takes over your life: drugs, food, sex, pornography, television, video games, social media, and so on.

Instead, Paul instructed us to be controlled by the Holy Spirit, not just once but daily, submitting our lives to Him every day.[12] How do you do that? The Bible provides three additional commands that, if obeyed, will ensure you're filled with the Spirit daily.

1. *Walk in the Spirit.* "I say, walk by the Spirit, and you will not carry out the desire of the flesh" (Gal. 5:16). The idea is to keep on walking in fellowship with the ways of the Holy Spirit. Just as fish need water to survive and you need air to survive, so you must depend on the Holy Spirit to survive this sinful world.
2. *Don't grieve the Spirit.* "Do not grieve the Holy Spirit of God, by whom you were sealed for the day of redemption" (Eph. 4:30). You grieve the Spirit whenever you deliberately sin. You delight the Spirit whenever you deliberately reject sin and live in holiness. When you do grieve the Spirit, you must seek immediate restoration through repentance.
3. *Don't quench the Spirit.* "Do not quench the Spirit" (1 Thess. 5:19). You quench the Spirit whenever you resist His attempts to produce Christ's likeness within you. You do this by consciously acting in selfish ways, demanding your own will and not Christ's will be done in your life. Again, when you do quench the Spirit, you must seek immediate restoration through repentance.

Principle #3: God's Power Is Amplified by His Word

One of the outworkings of being filled with the Holy Spirit is an increased desire to grow into maturity as a

Christian—to become more and more like Christ in character. To do that, Spirit-filled believers make it a daily habit to spend time with the Lord in His Word.

Hebrews 4:12 says, "The word of God is living and active and sharper than any two-edged sword, and piercing as far as the division of soul and spirit, of both joints and marrow, and able to judge the thoughts and intentions of the heart." It's more powerful than any soldier's sword because it can defeat Satan (Eph. 6:17), and it's more powerful than any surgeon's scalpel because it can cut to the soul, convicting sinners of sin (Acts 5:33; 7:54).

Spirit-filled believers make it a daily habit to spend time with the Lord in His Word.

According to Paul, "All Scripture is inspired by God [literally, "God-breathed"] and profitable for teaching, for reproof, for correction, for training in righteousness; so that the man of God may be adequate, equipped for every good work" (2 Tim. 3:16–17). Because God's Word is inspired, it is "profitable," serving four purposes in the life of the believer:

1. *Teaching*. The God-breathed content being taught and the manner in which it's taught—the consumption of the Word of power.
2. *Reproof*. The power of the Word to make you conscious of sin in your life, motivating you to get rid of it.

3. *Correction*. The positive side of reproof. The power of the Word "straightens us out" (v. 16 TLB), ensuring straight doctrine and deeds.
4. *Training*. The power of the Word to guide you away from a life of sin and toward a life of sanctification—being set apart as holy—so you might live "in righteousness" (v. 16).

Spending time in God's Word isn't merely an academic exercise; it's meant to be a practical exercise. In the words of a friend, "The Word of God supernaturally equips the man of God for the works of God."[13] That's what verse 17 is driving at.

Understand this very clearly: The Holy Spirit is no substitute for God's Word, and God's Word is no substitute for the Holy Spirit. They work together for the same goal: to mold us into the image of God's beloved Son, Jesus Christ. That holy partnership between the Word of God and the Spirit of God is what Paul had in mind when he wrote to the Ephesian Christians about "the washing of water [the Holy Spirit] with the word [the Bible]" to produce Christians who are "holy and blameless" (Eph. 5:26–27).

Principle #4: God's Power Is Often Accessed Through Prayer

We'll explore prayer in greater depth in chapter 3, but for now, it's enough to know that human prayer and divine power are mysteriously linked. While God can and does sometimes work apart from human intercession, there is a consistent relationship between our asking and God's answering.

Theologian Karl Barth said, "To clasp the hands in prayer is the beginning of an uprising against the disorder of the world."[14] And James said the prayer of a righteous man or woman releases great power (5:16). Abraham prayed and saved the city of Sodom from destruction—at least for a while, until not even ten righteous persons could be found in that wicked city (Gen. 18:23–33). And the man born blind, after he was healed by Jesus and then dragged into court to be interrogated by the Pharisees, told them, "We know that God does not hear sinners; but if anyone is God-fearing and does His will, He hears him" (John 9:31).

Human prayer and divine power are mysteriously linked.

When it comes to unleashing God's power in your life, these are the questions you must answer:

- *Am I a child of God?*
- *Am I being filled daily by the Spirit of God?*
- *Am I spending time in the Word of God?*
- *Am I praying to access the power of God?*

Answering no to any of these questions is likely to limit your experience of God's power in your life. However, when you can honestly answer yes to them, you can watch for the God of power to work miracles of power in your life when you need Him most.

CHAPTER 3

MIRACLES OF PROVISION

SOMETIMES INDIVIDUALS are the recipients of God's miraculous provision for a specific need they have. Such miracles not only meet a specific need for the individual but also serve as a reminder of God's power that they can recall when they face a future challenge.

But other times God demonstrates His power to an entire congregation of believers to meet a need and remind the church of His indescribable power. I'm privileged to be the pastor of a church that witnessed such a miracle more than fifteen years ago—a miracle God used to demonstrate His power to other churches throughout the nation.

When I arrived at First Baptist Church of Dallas in 2007, things at the church weren't looking good. Before I was called to be pastor, the church had had three previous pastors in just the last eighteen years. The people had become discouraged, the giving had diminished, and the buildings were in disrepair. To help turn things around, I told the members we were going to demolish six blocks of crumbling buildings and construct a brand-new campus in downtown Dallas that reflected the glory of God. It would be the largest single building project in modern church history: $130 million at the time. I believed God would provide all that was needed to complete the task if we would get behind the vision with prayerful persistence and sacrificial giving.

The congregation enthusiastically embraced the vision—but then came the recession of 2008, which lingered into 2009, the greatest economic downturn in America since the depression of the 1930s. I was convinced the Lord wanted us to move forward with the building project, but watching the stock market tumble made me queasy. Was my timing off? I remember in March 2009 the S&P Stock Index Fund reached an all-time low of 666, an ominous sign for a church! So the timing was in serious question. Should we cancel the project or at least pause it until the economy recovered? I didn't know what the Lord wanted us to do.

I called the chair of our building committee and my best friend since childhood, Mark Lovvorn, and shared with him my dilemma. Mark listened quietly and said, "Robert, I understand. All I know that we can do is pray." That night I could hardly sleep, just tossing and turning, thinking about it.

The next morning, I got down on my knees in my office and prayed, "Lord, I believe You have placed it in our hearts to build this worship center and campus for Your glory. I'm trying to obey You, but I just don't know what to do. If You want us to move forward, I need a sign from You—and I need it today."

Now, throughout my ministry, I've taught that we shouldn't seek God's direction through signs. But sometimes, when you're desperate enough, you do what you have to do! You need to understand that I was at the end of my spiritual rope.

I got up from my knees and went to a luncheon that had already been scheduled with a member of the building committee and her husband, Joan and Andy Horner, two of the most dedicated believers I've ever met and founders of the Premier Designs company. They had just returned from a mission trip to Argentina and were sharing with me about their trip. Nothing was said about the building project during our lunch, but as we started to leave, Andy made an offhand comment. "Pastor, I know times are difficult, but I think we need to move forward with the building program." At that moment, I silently asked the Lord, *Is this Your thumbs-up to go ahead? It doesn't seem like much of a sign, but I'll take anything You've got!*

I thanked Andy and Joan for their encouragement and walked to my car. Before returning to my office, I decided to stop at Baylor Hospital to see another church member. As I drove down St. Paul Street in downtown Dallas, Andy called me and said, "Pastor, there's something I forgot to tell you. Joan and I have decided to give the lead gift to the building effort." When Andy told me how much, I nearly jumped the curb. It was the largest amount of money anyone had ever given in our church's 140-year history! In fact, people in the church fundraising business told us they believed it was the largest amount of money ever given to a church by a single member.

I told Andy I couldn't believe it—me, the guy who had asked God just that morning for confirmation, the guy of little faith. I thanked Andy for their generosity. He said he and Joan had planned on giving it for six months, and he didn't know why they hadn't said anything before that day. I told him I knew exactly why: God used that gift to confirm His word to me and to encourage others to give.

Several other families, when they heard about the Horners' miraculous gift, stood up and said, "We want to be a part of this in a significant way." Then dozens and dozens of others, when they heard about it, said, "Yes, we believe God is in this." Today, we have a beautiful, modern campus in the heart of downtown Dallas that has greatly enhanced our ministry and is completely debt-free—all to the glory of God. Our campus has not only been a beacon for the gospel in Dallas but throughout the entire world.

In the years since that miracle, I have heard from dozens of church leaders around the world who have said, "We were in the same situation as your church. We had a vision, but the recession caused us to hesitate about going forward. But when we heard what God had done at First Baptist Dallas, it gave us the confidence to move forward in faith!"

Our Need for Provision

Sometimes we see God's provision in the rearview mirror—in hindsight, after the fact. And sometimes we see God's provision stretching out before us, like a straight road with signs along the way. That was the case in my desire to follow God's will regarding our building project. However God chooses to invade our lives, we can rest assured that He will care for our needs.

Because He made us, God—more than anyone (including ourselves)—knows exactly what we need and when we need it. The Lord knows we need certain things not only to sustain life but also to thrive in life. Let's look at three provisions we all need.

Physical Provision

Democratic presidential candidate Adlai Stevenson said, "Understanding human needs is half the job of meeting them."[1] What's implied in Stevenson's remark is that meeting human needs is made more difficult if we can't identify human needs, the most basic of which are for physical provision. Jesus addressed these needs in the Sermon on the Mount.[2]

First, *the need for food in our stomachs*. The Lord said, "Do not be worried about your life, as to what you will eat or what you will drink. . . . Look at the birds of the air, that they do not sow, nor reap nor gather into barns, and yet your heavenly Father feeds them" (Matt. 6:25–26).

Second, *the need for a shirt (or dress) on our backs*. In the same context, Jesus said, "Do not be worried about . . . your body, as to what you will put on. . . . Why are you worried about clothing? Observe how the lilies of the field grow; they do not toil nor do they spin, yet I say to you that not even Solomon in all his glory clothed himself like one of these. But if God so clothes the grass of the field, which is alive today and tomorrow is thrown into the furnace, will He not much more clothe you?" (vv. 25, 28–30).

Third, *the need for a roof over our heads*. Jesus doesn't specifically mention this (though it's implied in the context of Matthew 6), but we all know shelter is something we need to provide for ourselves and our loved ones—a place to find "rest and shelter for the night."[3]

Financial Provision

The saying "Money makes the world go round" may be hyperbolic, but there is a kernel of truth in it. Money is the means by which we purchase everything from the bread in our cupboards to an education for our children. Numerous surveys reveal that the primary cause of anxiety is a lack of money. Money's ability to produce feelings of security and contentment, along with its seeming power to determine the quality of life we experience, explains why there are so many warnings in Scripture about worshiping money. Jesus famously said, "You cannot worship God and money" (see Matt. 6:24). Why did He choose to name money rather than sex, jobs, or sports as a false god that could become a focus of our lives? Because money has a unique ability to control the course of our lives and, therefore, to consume our thoughts and affections.

The writer to the Hebrews instructed, "Make sure your character is free from the love of money, being content with what you have; for He Himself has said, 'I will never desert you, nor will I ever forsake you'" (13:5). It's a warning to heed because, as Paul wrote, "Those who want to get rich fall into temptation and a snare and many foolish and harmful desires which plunge men into ruin and destruction. For the love of money is a root of all sorts of evil, and some by longing for it have wandered away from the faith and pierced themselves with many griefs" (1 Tim. 6:9–10).

Yet we must have some money, if for nothing else to provide for our physical needs. After all, Paul also wrote, "If you don't work [to earn your daily bread], you don't eat" (2 Thess. 3:10 MSG).

Relational Provision

Not only do we have physical and financial needs but we also have a need for human relationships. Typically, this is provided for in two ways.

First, *someone to love*. We were made to love and be loved. For many of us, that means finding someone we can spend our lives with—a husband or a wife. After God created Adam from the dust of the ground and placed him in the garden of Eden, his only companions were the animals God created. As loving and loyal as a dog or cat may be, a pet cannot meet our deepest emotional needs and longings. Only another person can do that. That's why the Lord said, "It is not good for the man to be alone; I will make a helper suitable for him" (Gen. 2:18). However, it's important to note that marriage isn't the only means by which God meets our need for genuine, loving relationships. For those who are unmarried, God also fulfills this need by providing companionship through caring friendships with fellow believers.

Not only do we have physical and financial needs but we also have a need for human relationships.

Second, *a place to belong*. We were not only made to love and be loved but also made to live in community—to be a part of a family and to form bonds of friendship. In 1982, NBC aired a new comedy series set in a Boston bar: *Cheers*. What most people remember about the show is the chorus of the show's theme song: "Sometimes you wanna go / Where everybody knows your name / And they're always glad you came."[4]

As I wrote in my book *Invincible*, "At no time in the history of the world have we been more connected to one another" through social media and smart devices. Yet, "it's also ironic, because at no time in the history of the world have we been more disconnected from one another."[5] Social and civic organizations such as the Kiwanis Club, the Rotary, and the Lions Club have all seen a decline in memberships. And the church, where you'd think people could find a welcoming, loving, impactful community, is losing members. Church attendance has steadily declined since the turn of the twenty-first century and is lower today than it was before the COVID-19 pandemic.[6]

The Promise of Provision

None of the human needs we've discussed thus far will come as a surprise to you. Yet many people are skeptical of God's promise to provide for these very real needs.

We could look at any number of biblical passages that assure us of God's constant care for us, but we'll limit ourselves to just one: Psalm 145:14–16, which says, "The Lord sustains all who fall and raises up all who are bowed down. The eyes of all look to You, and You give them their food in due time. You open Your hand and satisfy the desire of every living thing."

We don't know when David composed this psalm. The title gives us no clue; it simply says "A Psalm of Praise, of David."[7] In this psalm, David praised God for His miracles, His mercy and grace, His everlasting kingdom, and His attention to those who cry out for provision. From the first to the last verse of Psalm 145, David affirmed that God is in control and can be counted on to meet our needs.

Verses 14–16 outline three promises the Lord makes to us:

1. *He sustains the downtrodden*—those in the dumps, kicked to the curb.
2. *He raises the oppressed*—those who are the maligned, the forgotten.
3. *He satisfies all who look to Him*—those who, in humility, turn to Him in faith.

I like what Warren Wiersbe wrote about these promises:

> Our great God is not an "absentee landlord" who collects rent but never repairs the roof. He knows our every need and He is there to help those who call on Him—those who fall, those carrying back-breaking burdens, those who hunger, and certainly those who want to be saved from their sins (Acts 2:21). We toil for our daily bread, but all God has to do is open His hand when He hears our cries and meet whatever need we have. When He supplies

one need, we must praise Him, and we must praise Him when He supplies the next need![8]

When was the last time the Lord met a need in your life? Can you trace His fingerprints on that situation? Did you praise Him? If not, why don't you pause your reading for a moment and thank God for His miraculous provision for you?

If you can't think of a need the Lord has met in your life, maybe you haven't turned to Him to ask Him to provide for your needs:

- Perhaps you've been going it alone, flying solo.
- Perhaps you see yourself as a pull-yourself-up-by-your-bootstraps type of Christian.
- Perhaps you view God as useful for the big stuff—sin and salvation—but for the small stuff, well, you're on your own. "God helps those who help themselves," after all. Right?

How's that working out for you? As I'm writing this, eggs have become so expensive you'd think all the chickens in the United States were laying gold. In fact, everything is more expensive these days. Many have had to make difficult choices, not necessarily between needs and wants but between this need and that need. If that's you, or if you know someone who fits this category, then read on with care because I'm going to give you some practical principles to guide you when asking for God's miraculous provision to meet your needs.

The Principles of Provision

Scripture points to at least four principles we should adopt when we're looking for God to provide for our needs.

The Principle of A.S.K.

James cut to the chase in explaining why so many of us never experience any supernatural answers to our prayers when he wrote, "You do not have because you do not ask" (4:2). How profoundly simple! Although God never promised to answer our every request, He rarely answers requests we've never made.

And when we do decide to take James's admonition to pray seriously, we need to follow the A.S.K. principle that James's half brother Jesus taught: *ask*, *seek*, and *knock*. Jesus said, "*Ask*, and it will be given to you; *seek*, and you will find; *knock*, and it will be opened for you. For everyone who asks receives, and he who seeks finds, and to him who knocks it will be opened" (Matt. 7:7–8).

Although God never promised to answer our every request, He rarely answers requests we've never made.

In the Greek language, the verbs "ask," "seek," and "knock" are present imperatives, meaning we're to do continuously what is commanded. We're to keep on asking, keep on seeking, and keep on knocking.

The principle of A.S.K. says, *Pray with persistence*. Or as Paul put it, "Pray without ceasing" (1 Thess. 5:17).

What's one need you have right now? Have you prayed about it? Are you still praying about it—asking, seeking, and knocking—or did your prayer consist of one and done?

One of the joys of becoming a grandparent is watching your grandchildren put your children through what they put you through: an incessant barrage of questions and appeals. They keep coming back, over and over, asking for this and that. Moms and dads may go into their room, close the door, and put in their AirPods to escape from the questions. But our heavenly Father never closes His door or puts in His AirPods to drown out our prayers. So, keep asking, keep seeking, keep knocking. Pray with persistence.

The principle of A.S.K. also says, *Pray with boldness*. When you come to the Lord with a request, don't be obnoxious and demanding—but don't be shy, kicking the dirt, and hemming and hawing. Come into the Lord's presence with boldness, as Paul said in Ephesians 3:12, and make your request known. I love how Eugene Peterson paraphrased Matthew 7:7–8 in *The Message*: "Don't bargain with God. Be direct. Ask for what you need. This isn't a cat-and-mouse, hide-and-seek game we're in." If you sincerely seek the Lord's will and boldly ask Him to intervene on your behalf, you'll receive what you've asked for, find what you've been seeking, and open the doors you've knocked on.

But there is one caveat: Your request must be according to God's will and for God's glory. Remember what James said about us not receiving because we haven't asked? Well, there's another reason God may not provide for our needs: "You ask and do not receive, because you ask with wrong motives, so that you may spend it on your pleasures" (James 4:3). God wants to meet your needs, but He might withhold a raise or promotion because He knows you intend to use that extra money to buy a boat or some other toy when that money should be used to fund your child's braces or education or to pay down a crushing debt.

Before Jesus laid out the principle of A.S.K. in the Sermon on the Mount, He said, "Do not worry then, saying, 'What will we eat?' or 'What will we drink?' or 'What will we wear for clothing?' . . . for your heavenly Father knows that you need all these things. But seek first His kingdom and His righteousness, and all these things will be added to you" (Matt. 6:31–33). What Jesus means by seeking God's kingdom and righteousness is that when we make it a priority to live on earth as if we are living in heaven, where God's will and God's glory are the most important things in life, then God will meet our earthly needs.

Jesus doubles down on that promise in Matthew 7:9–11: "What man is there among you who, when his son asks for a loaf, will give him a stone? Or if he asks for a fish, he will not give him a snake, will he? If you then, being evil [sinful], know how to give good gifts to your children, how much more will your [sinless] Father who is in heaven give what is good to those who ask Him!" When one of my grandchildren asks for a PB&J, I don't give them a peanut butter and jelly*fish* sandwich. In the same way, Jesus says, God the Father, who is more loving than any of us, will meet our needs if we put into practice the principle of A.S.K.

The Principle of Work

The next principle to experience God's miraculous provision in your life is the principle of work. You may be protesting, saying, "Pastor, are you saying that we have to work for our miraculous provisions?" Yes, many times the way God provides for what we need is through our labor. In Deuteronomy 8:18, God says, "You shall remember the LORD your God, for it is He who is giving you power to make wealth, that He may confirm His covenant which He swore to your fathers, as it is this day." Now, ultimately God is responsible for "every good thing given and every perfect gift" in our lives (James 1:17), but sometimes those gifts come through our work. As the old saying goes, "God gives us the strength to dig the ditch to earn the money to buy the bread to get the strength . . . to dig the ditch." God miraculously provides us the breath of life so we can provide for ourselves and our families.

In God's Word, there is a link between poverty and laziness. Now, understand me clearly: Some people can't work because of physical limitations or age restrictions, and we are to be gracious and helpful to them. However, for those who can work, there is a link between poverty and our choice to not work.

- "Laziness casts into a deep sleep, and an idle man will suffer hunger." (Prov. 19:15)

- "The sluggard does not plow after the autumn, so he begs during the harvest and has nothing." (Prov. 20:4)
- "The desire of the sluggard puts him to death, for his hands refuse to work; all day long he is craving, while the righteous gives and does not hold back." (Prov. 21:25–26)

In the New Testament, we see that the apostle Paul adopted the principle of work. In 2 Thessalonians 3:10, he said, "For even when we were with you, we used to give you this order: if anyone is not willing to work, then he is not to eat, either." That's the principle of work.

The Principle of Generosity

Let's be honest: Most of us would rather eat caviar instead of cabbage, wear Gucci instead of Goodwill, and drive a Mercedes instead of a Mazda. But God only promises to meet our needs, not our greeds. He's more than able to meet those needs because He has a storehouse of riches—that's the idea behind the promise of Philippians 4:19: "My God will supply all your needs according to His riches in glory in Christ Jesus." Since His riches are limitless and lavish, He gives lavishly and limitlessly.

This gets us to the principle of generosity, since God bestows blessings on us in proportion to the blessings we bestow on others. The context of verse 19 is one of generosity. In verse 15, Paul mentioned that the Philippians were the first and only believers to support his work after he left Macedonia. Then in verse 16, he praised them for sending two gifts while he ministered in Thessalonica. From there, in verses 17–18, Paul praised them for their financial generosity, which he said was like "a fragrant aroma, an acceptable sacrifice, well-pleasing to God" (v. 18).

The key passage on generosity, however, is 2 Corinthians 9:7, which says, "Each one must do just as he has purposed in his heart, not grudgingly or under compulsion, for God loves a cheerful giver."

Paul illustrated the principle that God bestows blessings on us in proportion to the blessings we bestow on others with a farmer sowing his seed. If he "sows sparingly," he will "reap sparingly" (v. 6). The farmer is free to sow as much or as little as he likes—doing "just as he has purposed in his heart" (v. 7). No one, not even the Lord, is telling you how generous you should be with your resources. That's up to you. Just realize the generosity of your hands starts with the generosity of your heart—and that's what God is ultimately interested in. So, Paul said don't be a *sad giver* ("grudgingly"), feeling sorrow for what you're giving up, and don't be a *mad giver* ("under compulsion"), feeling pressured to give. Rather, be a *glad giver* because the Lord "loves a cheerful giver" (v. 7). The Greek word translated as "cheerful" in this verse is *hilaron*, from which we get our word *hilarious*.

The late pastor and radio Bible teacher J. Vernon McGee once suggested that pastors lead their congregation in singing the doxology before taking the offering. Why? "This would put them in an attitude of giving and of giving joyfully. Also, they would be able to reach for their wallets as they stood up!"[9]

God loves to bless hilarious givers who give generously to His work of spreading the gospel throughout the world and who give generously to those who have greater needs than their own.

I don't know who coined this phrase, but it's true: "I cried because I had no shoes until I met a man who had no feet." Everywhere you look, there are people in need. What are you doing to meet someone's needs? The principle of generosity highlights the truth that God bestows blessings on us in proportion to the blessings we bestow on others.

On the heels of the 2008 recession, a friend was thrown out of work. The ministry he worked for had a shortfall in funding and cut its staff to survive. During that time of belt-tightening, with kids in college, while he was looking for work, the bottom of his water heater gave way. He didn't have the money to replace it. He ruled out robbing a bank, but he was either going to have to borrow the money from his family or take out a loan. Then a friend by the name of Ben called and said he was on his way to the house with something. When Ben showed up, he handed our mutual friend a check for $1,000. Ben said the Lord compelled him to give the money. That $1,000 was just enough to cover the cost of a new water heater and pay the plumber to install it.

The Principle of Refuge

When it comes to securing needed provisions for our lives, we've learned from Matthew 7:7–11 to practice the principle of A.S.K. and from Philippians 4:19 to practice the principle of generosity. But there's one more, which is found in Psalm 34:8–10: "O taste and see that the LORD is good; how blessed is the man who takes refuge in Him! O fear the LORD, you His saints; for to those who fear Him there is no want. The young lions do lack and suffer hunger; but they who seek the LORD shall not be in want of any good thing."

When we fear the Lord, He provides everything we need when we need it.

David probably composed this psalm after he disguised himself as a madman in the presence of "Achish king of Gath" (1 Sam. 21:10) and then fled to the cave of Adullam while running from King Saul, who sought to kill him.[10] In the verses we're concerned with, David articulated our final principle to seeing God meet our needs: the principle of refuge and reverence.

To "take refuge" in God (Ps. 34:8) means to trust in Him wholeheartedly. Unlike the young lion who trusts in its own strength and fails to make a kill and ends up hungry, the person who takes refuge in God will not be disappointed—or, as David put it in verse 10, will "not be in want of any good thing."

If you've ever lived in an area prone to tornadoes, then you know what a storm cellar is. When the warning sirens sound, you quickly go to a place that is designed to withstand the destructive winds. In the first church I pastored, there was a building across the street from our parsonage with a basement that had been designated as a tornado shelter. Every time the storm sirens sounded (for some reason it was always just as we were sitting down for dinner), we gathered our two little girls and headed across the street to that designated basement. We were always a little nervous when we heard the sirens, but once we were in the basement, we felt secure.

As taking refuge in God brings God's blessing, so does fearing God (v. 9). This isn't the kind of fear we have of getting a root canal. Rather, it's a sense of overwhelming reverence we have for the Lord, resulting in obedience to Him. When we fear the Lord, He provides everything we need when we need it.

All four of these principles were beautifully displayed in the faith of my older daughter, Julia, and her husband, Ryan, one evening after a worship service in London several years back. They had just suffered their third miscarriage and were struggling to understand the Lord's purpose for their lives as a couple who desired to be parents.

During the service, the speaker challenged the audience to list what they wanted God to do that was above and beyond anything that could naturally occur. That was an easy list for Julia and Ryan to make. They had been diligent in prayer—asking, seeking, knocking—and generous with their time and talents in working with students and their parents. But that evening, they turned to the Lord with complete trust and reverence for what He wanted for their lives, and they left convinced God wanted them to have children. So, they asked God to give them triplets—one life to replace each one lost.

When they told me what they were praying for, I, great man of faith that I am, said, "Oh, please, don't pray for that. You'll be disappointed. We don't have a history of multiple births in our family. You're setting yourselves up for heartache."

Julia said, "Dad, if you're going to see God do big things, you have to pray big things."

In December 2017, Julia delivered three precious and healthy children: Blair, Barrett, and Blake.[11] Every time I think of or see them, I'm reminded that God "is able to do far more abundantly beyond all that we ask or think" (Eph. 3:20).

What big thing do you want to see God provide in your life? Remember, He's ready and willing to provide above and beyond what you could possibly imagine.

CHAPTER 4

MIRACLES OF PROTECTION

DURING THE SUMMER of 1980, a friend went with his high school youth group on a mission trip to central Mexico to help a Christian school operated by José Pérez and his wife, Maria. The school was in the hills outside of the city. It consisted of several buildings—classrooms, dormitories, gymnasium, kitchen, and dining hall—protected behind a gated wall. My friend's youth group was there to repair buildings, clear brush from the enclosed compound, and clean rooms for the next school year.

At the time, Mexico was at war with the notorious Guadalajara cartel. At least once, the youth leaders had to bribe police officers to permit them to continue their journey south. When the group of students reached the school and settled in, Maria told them they should never go outside the gate unless accompanied by her or José. To drive her point home, she told a hair-raising story.

A few weeks earlier, with the school year ended and students and staff sent home, Maria had an appointment in the city. José was away. Maria knew she shouldn't make the trip alone, but she couldn't wait for her husband to return. Despite reports of an armed gang roaming the road that connected the school and the city, Maria committed her protection to the Lord. She left the compound in her car and started down the hill. She knew if anything happened, it would occur at a roadside shrine at the bottom of a blind rise.

Approaching the rise in the road, she slowed her car and prayed for God to protect her. Just as she crested the rise, she saw several young men armed with machine guns walk from the shrine into the middle of the street. One raised a hand and yelled for her to stop. She did. Her mind raced. Should she turn the car around and hurry back to the school compound? Or should she speed past the gang, hoping they'd jump out of the way? She couldn't just sit there, idling in her car. If she did, she was sure to be robbed, at best, and at worst . . . well, it was too horrible to contemplate.

Just as she was about to put the car into reverse, the gunmen lowered their weapons and looked as if they'd seen something frightening. They turned and ran into the thick jungle paralleling the road.

Maria made it into the city without incident, but she feared she might encounter the same armed men or others on her way back to the school. So again, she asked for the Lord's protection. And she praised Him when she came upon the spot next to the roadside shrine, where the gang had stopped her before, to see that the road was empty.

A week later, Maria was talking with a friend. She told Maria about a gang of hoodlums who came running into the city, breathless and scared. They were passing the word that others should avoid the road leading from the school to the city. They said they had stopped a woman on that road with the intention of robbing her and perhaps assaulting her. But as their leader began approaching the car, the gang saw a man sitting in the passenger seat they hadn't seen before. There was something about the passenger's presence that unnerved them and sent them running in fear into the jungle. Maria asked when that was. When her friend told her, Maria felt awe and praise for the greatness of God, who had protected her.

Apparently, God dispatched one of His holy angels to ride shotgun with Maria that day. Maria never saw him, but when the armed gang showed signs of intending to harm one of God's precious daughters, the angel revealed himself, and the thugs saw him—and ran in fear.

Our Need for Protection

No matter where we live, dangers surround us. As one man said, "However well organized the foundations of life may be, life must be full of risks."[1] And so it is.

Paul said something similar in 2 Timothy 3:1: "Realize this, that in the last days difficult times will come." When Paul referred to "difficult times," he wasn't talking about daily inconveniences; he was talking about clear and present dangers. The Greek word translated as "difficult" is *chalepos*. It's used only one other time in the New Testament, in Matthew 8:28, where it describes two demon-possessed men as "extremely violent." Paul was describing days that are fierce and menacing—filled with pitfalls. That certainly describes the days in which we live, in which we can face physical and spiritual dangers.

Physical Dangers

No one knows what a day may bring (Prov. 27:1). A storm may roll through and damage your property—or destroy it in a hurricane or tornado. Lightning might strike your house, or a wire in a light switch might spark a fire that burns your home to the ground. You may wake up tomorrow and feel a lump that wasn't there the day before. You might receive a phone call from somebody informing you that a loved one has been in a terrible accident.

One of the most meaningful miracles of protection in my own life happened when I was young. My father worked for Braniff International Airlines. As a result, we received free passes for the family to travel—on standby. I tell people I've slept in the best airports in the world while waiting to get on a flight. When I was about four or five, my father flew from Dallas to Houston for the day. On his return flight later that afternoon, he had a confirmed seat—that is, until a last-minute paying passenger showed up. My dad was bumped and had to catch another flight. Forty-three minutes after takeoff, the plane my father was to be on crashed near Buffalo, Texas, killing everyone on board.

David says in Psalm 139:16, "In Your book were all written the days that were ordained for me, when as yet there was not one of them." It's not the purpose of this book to wrestle with all the theological questions one could ask about why God chose to spare my father's life and not the life of the man who took his seat, to say nothing of the rest of the passengers on that plane. God, in His wisdom and providence from eternity past, made that choice. It simply wasn't my father's time to go. As it was, my father didn't live a long life, but it was a significant life. Without his involvement in my spiritual development, it's doubtful I'd be in ministry today.

I hope you're just as grateful to the Lord for His providence in your life as I am that my dad lost his seat that day.

You likely also have a story of God's miracle of protection—either in your life or in the life of someone you know. I hope you're just as grateful to the Lord for His providence in your life as I am that my dad lost his seat that day.

A colleague once told me about his friend, Todd, who was driving on a highway behind an eighteen-wheeler with a load strapped to its flatbed. While the truck was racing down the road at seventy-five miles an hour, one of the straps snapped. The buckle end of the strap hit the pavement and ricocheted into Todd's front windshield, hit the passenger seat, and came to rest in the back of his SUV. If someone had been in that passenger seat, the buckle would have hit them in the head, severely injuring or killing them. If the buckle had hit a foot or two toward the driver's side, Todd probably wouldn't be here to tell the tale.

Whether because of natural disasters, accidents, criminal activity, or warfare, physical dangers are simply part and parcel of living in a fallen world.

Spiritual Dangers

Spiritual dangers are even more inevitable . . . and dangerous. No one said it better than the apostle Paul: "Be strong in the Lord and in the strength of His might. Put on the full armor of God, so that you will be able to stand firm against the schemes of the devil. For our struggle is not against flesh and blood, but against the rulers, against the powers, against the world forces of this darkness, against the spiritual forces of wickedness in the heavenly places" (Eph. 6:10–12).

Secular humanism, materialism, spiritualism, atheism, the occult, false religions, and any number of other -isms and falsehoods are at war with the gospel of Jesus Christ. This war is for the souls of unbelieving men and women. Paul said of Satan, "The god of this world has blinded the minds of the unbelieving so that they might not see the light of the gospel of the glory of Christ, who is the image of God" (2 Cor. 4:4).

However, spiritual dangers are not just reserved for unbelievers. Believers are also in Satan's crosshairs. He sows discord among Christian brothers and sisters, doubts in the minds of believers, and distractions to keep us busy with the things of the world so we won't attend to the things of the Spirit.

Some of us have come to faith in Jesus out of a false religion, and we know firsthand the spiritual dangers that lurk in the dark corners of anti-Christian philosophies. Others of us have grown up in the church, perhaps coming to faith at an early age. Yet being in a church doesn't immunize us against personal struggles with immorality, greed, or placing our own needs and preferences above those of other Christians in the church, which always results in friction and factions.

The Promise of God's Protection

Though dangers surround us and may spring upon us suddenly, we aren't defenseless. God repeatedly encourages us to pray for His protection against every kind of danger we can imagine.

In Psalm 22, David pleaded with God, "Deliver my soul from the sword, my only life from the power of the dog. Save me from the lion's mouth; from the horns of the wild oxen You answer me" (vv. 20–21).

One Sunday a few years ago, I was teaching Psalm 22, and I explained to the congregation that David was praying for protection from the common sources of danger in his day: warfare, animal attacks, and accidents. I said that if David were praying that prayer today, he might say something like, "Lord, deliver me from muggers, from drive-by shootings, and from those SUVs whirring by me on the freeway." After the first service, I was handed a note from one of our members, who had apparently misheard me. I read the note aloud during the next service: "Dear Pastor, I couldn't agree with you more. I can't stand those SOBs that whiz by me on the freeway!"

Scripture is filled with promises of God's protection. Let's look at another psalm for protection penned by King David. Psalm 121 is described as "A Song of Ascents," so called because Jews who traveled to Jerusalem to worship had to ascend Mount Moriah to reach the temple, which was on top of the mountain. The word *keep*, or its equivalent, is used six times in these eight verses, making this a psalm of protection. Since the hills around Jerusalem provided perfect cover for bandits, it was foolish to travel the roads alone, so pilgrims traveled in groups. But bandits weren't the only dangers. Roads were rocky and could be slick if wet, so stumbling and falling was always a possibility. If you traveled a long distance to reach Jerusalem during the summer months, sunstroke was a risk. Even during the summer, nights could be bone-chilling and inhospitable to pilgrims. So, to remind themselves of God's care, Jews traveling to Jerusalem declared four truths about God in this psalm they could bank on.

First, *God is sovereign.* "I will lift up my eyes to the mountains," the psalmist wrote. "From where shall my help come? My help comes from the LORD, who made heaven and earth" (vv. 1–2). The phrase "heaven and earth" is the Hebrew equivalent of "from A to Z." It represents the totality of everything made.[2] What's so important about this? As Paul put it in Colossians 1:16, "By Him all things were created, both in the heavens and on earth, visible and invisible, whether thrones or dominions or rulers or authorities." If God made everything, then He is all-knowing, all-wise, and all-powerful. And if that's true, then there's nothing to fear from bandits who hide in the hills.

Second, *God is awake.* The late Christian businesswoman Mary Carter Crowley was a member of our church and encouraged untold numbers of people around the world with her strong Christian message. She once said, "Every evening, I turn my worries over to God. He's going to be up all night anyway."

God is eternally awake, and His eyes are constantly watching over His children. David declared, "The eyes of the LORD are toward the righteous" (Ps. 34:15). Because He's always looking after us, "He will not allow your foot to slip" (121:3) or stumble on rocky roads.[3] The psalmist emphasized God's care for us by saying, "He who keeps you will not slumber. Behold, He who keeps Israel will neither slumber nor sleep" (vv. 3–4). God "keeps" us by looking out for us, taking care of us, guarding and protecting us—even in something as simple as traveling.

God "keeps" us by looking out for us, taking care of us, guarding and protecting us—even in something as simple as traveling.

Third, *God is a shelter*. In verse 5, the psalmist reiterate, "the LORD is your keeper." He went on to say that the Lord is our shelter: "The LORD is your shade on your right hand. The sun will not smite you by day, nor the moon by night" (vv. 5–6). God shades us from the burning sun and warms us during the cool night. He is with us through the changes and challenges of life, sheltering us from harm both day and night, from the rising of the sun to the rising of the moon—from day to day, month to month, year to year. Whether by day or by night, in heat or in cold, the Lord is a constant shelter to protect us and provide all we need.

Does that mean that nothing bad ever happens to Christians? We know better than that! Hard things—very hard things—come into our lives. (I'm facing one of those hard things as I type these words.) But whether it is illness, broken relationships, terminations, or any other malady, we know that God protects His children from anything that is not part of His plan—a good plan—for our lives.

The late Donald Grey Barnhouse wrote,

> There is no will or act of creatures, men, angels or demons that can do other than work for our good. No dog can bark against us, no man can act or speak against us, no sinister power of evil can be against us, but all must be for our good. There is no phenomenon of nature—fire, flood, storm, earthquake—that can work us ultimate ill. The law of gravity cannot trip us up or cause anything to fall on us unless it has first been sifted through the will of God's purpose for our good.[4]

The righteous have no reason to be afraid of dangers because "he who dwells in the shelter of the Most High will abide in the shadow of the Almighty" (Ps. 91:1).

Fourth, *God is a shield*. Warren Wiersbe said, "We need not fear life or death, today or tomorrow, time or eternity, for we're in the loving care of the Father."[5] There's no evil design, whether conceived by armed criminals or by Satan, that God cannot shield us from as we go about our daily lives. And if by His will He allows us to suffer some evil, we must never forget that "God causes all things to work together for good to those who love God, to those who are called according to His purpose" (Rom. 8:28).

I recently read a story my friend Derrick Jeter wrote about a canoeing accident on a Texas river that threatened to take the lives of two of his children and how the Lord spared them. Derrick wrote,

> On a canoe trip with family and friends, now almost twenty years gone, the river ran swift. My oldest son, who at the time was perhaps ten or eleven years old, was in the bow of my canoe. I was in the stern and my daughter, who was six or seven years old, sat in the middle. Navigating a tricky rapid, we needed to keep right of a large boulder to find smooth water. My wife and second son, along with friends in other canoes, made it through safely. We didn't. Fearing we might lodge on the large rock, I pulled Cierra into my lap and tried to maneuver my paddle around her head. I couldn't bite the angry current quickly enough, and Derrick [my son] wasn't strong enough to swing our canoe wide. We struck center rock and center canoe, and stuck tight as the Brazos capsized my little family. I held onto Cierra and found a footing on the river bottom and came up spitting river water. I placed her on top of the boulder, out of the ravages of the river's swift stream. Derrick had disappeared.
>
> He remained underwater. Then he popped up like a cork downriver and was pulled into a friend's canoe—healthy and happy for the adventure he just had. I was overcome with gratitude and relief.
>
> That evening, I didn't sleep. I shuddered throughout the night, tears streaming down my temples, as my mind

> replayed the events just before the watery darkness washed over us and the terror of not seeing my towheaded boy. . . . I turned in the bed of my tent, my wife sleeping peacefully beside me, and praised the Lord of heaven and earth—the Lord of the Brazos—that my little boy, who had vanished from my sight and sound, was there sleeping next to his brother and sister.[6]

Was it coincidence, luck, or fate that saved Derrick's kids that day? Or was it God's providential hand that protected them? I've often heard my friend David Jeremiah say, "God's man in the center of God's will is immortal until God is finished with him."[7] I believe this is true. So did Paul. During his sermon before the Jews in Antioch, he said, "David, after he had served the purpose of God in his own generation, fell asleep, and was laid among his fathers and underwent decay" (Acts 13:36).

The Means of God's Protection

The Lord uses three primary means to demonstrate miracles of protection on our behalf: direct fortification, angelic intervention, and the Holy Spirit's direction. As we look at each one, we'll discover a practical application.

Direct Fortification

If you've spent any time in church, then you've likely heard of the "hedge of protection," asking God to surround someone with a protective barrier shielding them against harm, danger, and spiritual attacks. I remember my parents praying that God would place a hedge of protection around me when I traveled on mission trips and to college, and Amy and I have prayed many times for God's hedge of protection around our daughters and grandchildren.

Christian comedian Tim Hawkins has a funny bit about those who pray for a hedge of protection. He says, "A hedge, huh? I don't mean to complain, but is that really the best you can do? How about praying a thick cement wall with some razor wire on top of that bad boy? A hedge of protection sounds like it is one good pair of clippers away from being removed—and I'm sure the devil's got a pair of those lying around the old Sheol Shed."[8]

What you might not know is that this idea of a hedge of protection comes from the lips of Satan himself. When he appeared before the Lord, Satan said about Job, "Does Job fear God for nothing? Have You not made a hedge about him?" (Job 1:9–10). Of course, Satan wasn't referring to shrubbery. He was referring to God's direct fortification over Job, protecting his person ("a hedge about him"), his family ("a hedge about . . . his house"), and his possessions ("a hedge about . . . all he has"). Notice, Satan says the Lord's protection is "on every side"—before, behind, beside, below, and above—just as the Scripture promises: "As the mountains surround Jerusalem, so the LORD surrounds His people" (Ps. 125:2).

Speaking of mountains, in Psalm 18:2, David called God "my rock, in whom I take refuge," referring to his trust in God's immovable and eternal nature.[9] Man-made fortresses may crumble, but God is our "everlasting Rock"

(Isa. 26:4). He stands sure and solid today and tomorrow and forever. He is our fortress and place of refuge, a trusted fortification where we can find shelter, which leads to the practical application: *Place all that you are and all that you have into the hands of God, trusting Him with your life and the lives of your loved ones.*

I remember one day, many years ago, I left the church a few minutes early to get a haircut. On my way to the barbershop, I had just driven through an intersection when I heard the terrible screeching sound of brakes and then a huge crash. I looked in my rearview mirror, and the driver behind me had followed me through that intersection and had been broadsided by a car running a red light. His car was decimated. I pulled over to the side of the road and called 911 immediately, but it was too late. The driver was dead.

Place all that you are and all that you have into the hands of God, trusting Him with your life and the lives of your loved ones.

I went home that night and thought, *What if I had left work ten seconds later than I did? What if the pressure of my foot on the accelerator was a little lighter than it had been?* That would have greatly impacted my life. I'm not at all suggesting that God loved me more than He loved the driver who was killed. Instead, I'm saying that things I thought were my choices really weren't my choices. They were a part of God's plan for my life. And God has a plan for your life as well.

"Trust in the LORD with all your heart," Solomon advised, "and do not lean on your own understanding" (Prov. 3:5). You and I can trust in the Lord. There's nothing to fear because our God is the Rock who provides a hedge around us, our families, and our possessions. On a scale of 1 to 10, how high is your trust meter? What do you need to do to increase it a notch or two?

Angelic Intervention

The writer to the Hebrews warned his readers, "Do not neglect to show hospitality to strangers, for by this some have entertained angels without knowing it" (13:2). That was true of Maria Pérez on the road in central Mexico. And for all we know, that was equally true of Todd when that buckle crashed through his windshield or of Derrick's children on that canoe trip or of me on my way to the barbershop.

When the temple guards came to arrest Jesus in the garden of Gethsemane, Peter drew his sword to protect the Lord, which was a comically pathetic act, thinking *he* could protect God in the flesh. Jesus told Peter, "Put your sword back into its place. . . . Do you think that I cannot appeal to My Father, and He will at once put at My disposal more than twelve legions of angels?" (Matt. 26:52–53). That's seventy-two thousand angels!

Those same angels are available to protect you and me—to harass our spiritual enemies (Ps. 35:4–5), to deliver us from the wicked (Isa. 63:9), and to preserve us until we reach the final victory over this sinful world (Heb. 1:14).

One of the greatest biblical examples of this occurred in the life of the Old Testament prophet Elisha.

When the king of Syria learned that Elisha could miraculously discern his battle plans (2 Kings 6:11–12), the king sent a detachment of soldiers to Dothan to capture God's prophet (v. 14)—as if Elisha couldn't see that coming. In the morning, when Elisha's servant went outside, he saw the Syrian "army with horses and chariots . . . circling the city" (v. 15).

Frightened, he ran back inside and notified Elisha, who said, "Do not fear, for those who are with us are more than those who are with them" (v. 16). His servant must have thought, *Are you crazy?* That's why Elisha prayed, "O LORD, I pray, open his eyes that he may see" (v. 17). Back outside, "the LORD opened the servant's eyes and he saw; and behold, the mountain was full of horses and chariots of fire all around Elisha" (v. 17).

Billy Graham tells a similar story of a missionary couple in the New Hebrides Islands, John and Margaret Paton. Hostile natives surrounded their headquarters, intending to burn it to the ground and kill the missionaries as they came out. Before the tribesmen torched their home, John and Margaret prayed for God's protection. They prayed all night, waiting for the flames to engulf their home. But when daylight came, their house still stood, and the hostiles were gone. Their prayer turned to praise.

A year later, the chief of the tribe committed his life to Christ. John asked the chief about that night a year before—why hadn't the chief's men torched the house and killed John and Margaret? The chief said, "Who were all the men you had with you there?" John answered, "There were no men there, just my wife and I." No, the chief said, he and his tribesmen had seen many men standing guard. Hundreds of big men, he said, wearing shining garments with swords in their hands. They encircled the mission, and the natives were afraid to attack. It was then John realized that, because of their pleas for help, God had dispatched an angelic army to protect him and Margaret.[10]

When faced with danger, our first response shouldn't be fight or flight but prayer.

This gets us to the practical application: *When faced with danger, our first response shouldn't be fight or flight but prayer*. When Peter was imprisoned by Herod Agrippa in the Antonia Fortress, guarded by a quadruple guard of Roman soldiers, "the church of God" knelt in fervent prayer (Acts 12:5). God heard that prayer and sent an angel to rescue Peter and bring him safely to where they were meeting (vv. 6–17). A Puritan preacher named Thomas Watson said of this miraculous rescue, "The angel fetched Peter out of prison, but it was prayer that fetched the angel."[11]

Whenever we focus on dangers, we magnify them, increasing our fear. We need to magnify God, who not only possesses unlimited power to protect us from danger but also commands legions of angels who, at a moment's notice, can be dispatched from His side to surround us and shield us from physical and spiritual threats.

Remember the promise of Romans 8:31: "If God is for us, who is against us?" Ask the Lord to open your eyes to His sovereign power when the next trouble or danger crosses your path. That's the kind of prayer He loves to answer. You may not see one of His angels standing beside you, but you will see God more clearly.

The Holy Spirit's Direction

On the final night Jesus spent with His disciples before His crucifixion, He said He was going away "to prepare a place" for them (John 14:2). He encouraged them not to be troubled by His absence because "I will ask the Father, and He will give you another Helper, that He may be with you forever" (v. 16). It was the promise of the indwelling of the Holy Spirit, who would come just like Jesus and remain with them forever.[12]

The Greek word translated as "Helper" is *parakletos* and literally means "called alongside" or "called to one's aid." The word is often translated as "Comforter," which can come off as sounding as if the Holy Spirit is inferior to Christ and limited to only sympathizing with our sorrow.

Nothing could be further from the truth. The Spirit is equally divine with God the Father and God the Son, and His ministry is vast and varied, including guiding us (Rom. 8:14), strengthening us (Eph. 3:16), and empowering us against spiritual dangers (6:10–11). Bible teacher William Barclay says, "*Comforter* was once a perfectly good translation. It actually goes back to John Wycliffe, the first person to use it in his translation made in the fourteenth century. But in his day, it meant much more than it does now. The word came from the Latin *fortis*, which means *brave*; and a comforter was someone who enabled some dispirited creature to be brave."[13]

Courage in the face of danger is one of the great gifts of the Holy Spirit. The apostle Paul admonished Timothy, "God has not given us a spirit of timidity, but of power and love and discipline" (2 Tim. 1:7). God the Holy Spirit—who comes alongside us to protect us—is the source of that power.

David experienced the power and encouragement of the Holy Spirit many times during difficult and dangerous days. He wrote in Psalm 23, "Even though I walk through the valley of the shadow of death, I fear no evil, for You are with me; Your rod and Your staff, they *comfort* me"—in other words, they strengthen or encourage him (v. 4).

God the Holy Spirit—who comes alongside us to protect us—is the source of that power.

The Holy Spirit can protect us from danger, which leads us to the practical application: *Surrender control of our lives to the Holy Spirit* (Eph. 5:18), *walk closely with Him, listen for His "still small voice"* (1 Kings 19:12 KJV), *and obey His warnings about dangers ahead.*

The moment we trust in Christ as our Savior, we receive the gift of the Holy Spirit of God. In 1 Corinthians 12:13, Paul declared, "For by one Spirit we were all baptized into one body." Let's be clear, the Holy Spirit is not a power or a force. He is a Person whose presence in our lives results in all kinds of benefits, including power in times of temptation, encouragement in times of challenge, comfort in times of distress, and direction in times of confusion.

It is that last benefit I want to focus on briefly: *direction in times of confusion*. Although the Holy Spirit is a Person, He works as an internal GPS—leading us always in the direction of God's will, which is the safest place any person can be! In fact, the apostle Paul claimed that one of the best types of evidence of our salvation is the supernatural direction the Holy Spirit provides. He said, "For all who are being led by the Spirit of God, these are the sons of God" (Rom. 8:14). We can conclude that those who are *not* being led by the Spirit are not the children of God.

Frankly, there are many Christians who possess the presence of the Holy Spirit in their lives, but they are not benefiting from the power, encouragement, and strength the Holy Spirit offers. They don't realize there are some things we must do to experience the benefits of the Holy Spirit's presence in our lives.

For example, Paul instructed the Galatian believers to "walk by the Spirit" (Gal. 5:16, 25), to be "led by the Spirit" (v. 18), and to "live by the Spirit" (v. 25). To help understand how to do this, picture a giant generator at the bottom of a hydroelectric dam. The generator is already there, but to move the blades of the generator's turbines, there are four concrete conduits above that generator through which thousands of gallons of water per minute must flow to activate the turbines. If we close any of those conduits, the generator will not work effectively.

The Holy Spirit is like that generator. He is always present in us, but there are four conduits that activate His power in us: the Bible, prayer, the church, and obedience to God.

First, *develop a plan for reading the Bible regularly*. Select a Bible translation or paraphrase that speaks to you. Don't race through your reading of God's Word in order to finish reading the Bible in a year. The Bible took fifteen hundred years to write, so why do we feel like we must rush through it in a year?

Second, *set an appointed time to talk with God through prayer*. The Bible instructs us to "pray without ceasing" (1 Thess. 5:17), meaning that prayer should be as natural and frequent as breathing. Prayer can be an ongoing conversation with God: As soon as we awaken in the morning, before we drift off to sleep at night, as we drive down the freeway (watch out for those SUVs!), and before we enter a difficult meeting, we can talk with our heavenly Father. But there can and should be a time that we have an "appointment" with God—a set time and place we kneel before our Creator to confess our sins, express gratitude for His goodness, and pour out our requests.

Third, *attend and serve in a church regularly*. Church participation is not optional for any believer who wants to experience the comfort, encouragement, and leadership of the Holy Spirit. Many times, those benefits flow into our lives through other Christians in the church. That's why the author of Hebrews linked hope, faithfulness, and encouragement to participation in a local church: "Let us hold fast the confession of our hope without wavering, for

He who promised is faithful; and let us consider how to stimulate one another to love and good deeds, not forsaking our own assembling together, as is the habit of some, but encouraging one another; and all the more as you see the day drawing near" (Heb. 10:23–25).

Finally, *obey what you know to be true*. Paul gave this pointed five-word warning in 1 Thessalonians 5:19: "Do not quench the Spirit." Nothing extinguishes the power of the Holy Spirit any more than disobedience to God's commands. What is one thing in your life you're doing that you know God wants you to stop doing? What is one thing you're not doing that you know God wants you to start doing?

There's an old saying: "Light obeyed bringeth light. Light rejected bringeth the night." We should never expect the Holy Spirit to provide more direction in our lives if we are not following the direction He has already provided for us.

We should never expect the Holy Spirit to provide more direction in our lives if we are not following the direction He has already provided for us.

No one understood that truth better than King David. During the period of time when he refused to repent of his sins of adultery and murder, David felt God's heavy hand upon him. He experienced the misery and terror of living outside of God's will and apart from God's blessing. But after he repented and accepted God's forgiveness for his sins, David was determined never to live outside of God's will again, which is why he prayed, "Search me, O

God, and know my heart; try me and know my anxious thoughts; and see if there be any hurtful way in me, and lead me in the everlasting way" (Ps. 139:23–24).

That's a good prayer for anyone who wants to experience God's miraculous protection.

CHAPTER 5

MIRACLES OF HEALING

THE YEAR I TURNED SIXTEEN was a significant one in my life. I experienced an overwhelming closeness with the Lord, having just acknowledged and surrendered to God's call to full-time vocational ministry. Yet no sooner had I committed my life to the Lord's call than He placed me under a severe test.

I was preparing for an upcoming mission trip to San Juan, Puerto Rico, at school's end. Just before our youth group was set to leave, inexplicably, my right arm became paralyzed. I felt nothing at all. It became all but useless. My parents took me to a neurologist. He ran tests and drew blood and performed whatever else neurologists do to determine the cause of paralysis—and found nothing. Medically, nothing seemed wrong with me. There was no physical reason my right arm, from shoulder to fingertips, should be completely numb.

With a shrug of the shoulder and a scratch of the head, the doctor saw no reason I couldn't go on the mission trip; I'd just have to do everything left-handed. It was a frightening time. I decided that going to San Juan to minister to others was better than sitting at home in Dallas with nothing but my increasing anxiety.

We arrived in San Juan without incident and began ministering there. The days were busy, and learning to get by with only my left hand was frustrating, but after a while

I stopped focusing on my paralyzed arm. The nights were another matter, though, and they became increasingly difficult to bear. So, one night as I was getting ready for bed, I cried out to the Lord to heal me—to bring feeling and mobility back into my right arm. I lay on my bed and put into practice Jesus's admonition in Matthew 7:7 to ask, seek, and knock, pleading with the Lord until I finally fell asleep. Later that night, I suddenly woke up. At first, I didn't notice it, then it dawned on me that I could feel and move my right arm. I praised God through tears and went back to sleep.

The next day, I called home with the exciting news. My dad praised the Lord with me and then told me my mother was in the hospital for a procedure. Later that day, I called my mom's hospital room to check on her and tell her the great news. She asked what time the paralysis had left, and I told her the approximate time in San Juan. She said that Dr. Criswell, our pastor, had paid her a visit and that she had asked him to pray for me because my arm was paralyzed and the doctors couldn't figure out why. Dr. Criswell prayed with my mother at the same hour, Dallas time, that my arm was healed in San Juan.

I'm skeptical of faith healers, but I firmly believe in faith healing—that our great and good God, according to His purposes, can heal us.

As mentioned earlier, I'm skeptical of faith healers, but I firmly believe in faith healing—that our great and good God, according to His purposes, can heal us. I have experienced

His divine invasion in my life with a miracle of physical healing. Perhaps you have, too, or maybe someone you love has received physical healing. If so, I encourage you to praise God regularly for His grace and mercy in your life.

While preparing for this chapter, I stumbled on an interview my friend Lee Strobel did with pastor Roger Olson. Strobel summarizes a point Olson made: "Many American evangelicals have relegated the supernatural and miraculous to the past (biblical times) and elsewhere (mission field) rather than seeing them as an ever-present possibility in their lives." Strobel then quotes Olson: "This is obvious from the way we react when someone gets sick. Of course, we pray for them, but what do we ask? That God would comfort them in the midst of their suffering. That God would guide the hands of surgeons. That God would give doctors wisdom and discernment. What's missing?" Strobel answers: "Asking God to supernaturally heal them." "Precisely," Olson says. "The Bible says to pray for their healing, lay hands on them, and anoint them with oil, but mainstream evangelicals tend to look down their noses at churches that do that."[1]

I'll have more to say about what the Bible prescribes for the sick later in this chapter, but I'm so grateful my mother and pastor asked the Lord to heal me directly.

The Need for Physical Healing

In the United States, physical health and wellness are big business. According to the Global Wellness Institute, the

US is the largest wellness market in the world, valued at $1.8 trillion.[2] You can hardly turn around without bumping into a gym or a commercial for weight loss.

I think what drives much of this is fear—the fear of getting older and losing our looks and ability to do what we could when we were younger. It reminds me of the story of a Florida couple who wanted to marry. Jacob was ninety-two, and Rebecca was eighty-nine. As they discussed their upcoming nuptials, they passed a drugstore and decided to go in. Speaking to the pharmacist, Jacob said, "We're getting married."

"Wow. That's great," the pharmacist said. "Congratulations."

Jacob asked, "Do you sell heart medication?"

"Yes, we do," the pharmacist said.

"How about medicine for circulation?"

"All kinds."

"Medicine for rheumatism?"

"Definitely."

"Medicine for memory loss, arthritis, jaundice?"

"Yes, many brands. Whatever the doctor orders."

"What about vitamins, sleeping pills, and Geritol?"

"Absolutely."

"And wheelchairs and walkers?"

"All speeds and sizes."

"Great," Jacob said. "We'd like to use your store as our wedding registry!"[3]

You may laugh now. But live long enough, and your laughter might turn to tears. Just look at Solomon's description of getting older in Ecclesiastes 12. Solomon admonished us in verses 1–2 to "Remember also [our] Creator in the days of [our] youth, before the evil days come and the years draw near when [we] will say, 'I have no delight in them'; before the sun and the light, the moon and the stars are darkened, and clouds return after rain."

Remember the old joke about old age? "Two things immediately go when you get old. The first is your memory. The second is . . ."

That's what Solomon's metaphor of sun, light, moon, and stars represents—the darkening of our mental capacity when we begin to think more slowly and our memory starts to slip. For many who are aging, this dimming of the mind results in depression, what Solomon called "clouds" and "rains"—that Eeyore-like feeling that your days are perpetually dismal and damp.

How else can I encourage you today?

Solomon wasn't finished with his description of old age, and it didn't get any better. In verses 3–5, he used the metaphor of a house and references to nature to represent how our bodies break down with age:

1. *The watchmen of the house tremble* pictures the shaking of the hands and arms.
2. *Mighty men stoop* refers to unsure knees and legs.
3. *The grinding ones stand idle because they are few* is an image for tooth loss.
4. *Those who look through windows grow dim* refers to weakening eyesight.

5. *The doors on the street are shut as the sound of the grinding mill is low* speaks of becoming hard of hearing.
6. *One will arise at the sound of the bird* is an image of rising with the roosters.
7. *All the daughters of song will sing softly* suggests losing control over the voice.
8. *Men are afraid of a high place and of terrors in the road* refers to the fear of falling.
9. *The almond tree blossoms* indicate graying.
10. *The grasshopper drags himself along* is an image of walking slowly.
11. *The caperberry is ineffective* is a reference to an ancient aphrodisiac and the loss of sexual drive.

Benjamin Franklin wrote, "In this world nothing can be said to be certain, except death and taxes."[4] It's ironic he didn't include *old age* since, at the time, Franklin was an eighty-three-year-old man suffering from gout, a large bladder stone, and pleurisy.

"Frail children of dust, and feeble as frail," is how the hymnist Robert Grant described the human condition.[5] In the Old Testament, Job's friend Eliphaz put it like this: "Man was born for trouble, as sparks fly upward" (Job 5:7). Part of that trouble comes in the guise of illness and injury.

I've titled this chapter "Miracles of Healing" with the understanding that the word *healing* is not limited only to our bodies but encompasses the whole person. The ancient Greeks viewed humans as separate parts: body, soul, and spirit. By and large, we've adopted that approach in Western cultures today. However, the ancient Hebrews viewed humans as whole beings. They taught that physical pain affects the spirit—what we might call mental and emotional health—and that spiritual pain affects physical health.

The word healing is not limited only to our bodies but encompasses the whole person.

A sinful world produces sickness and suffering, whether physically, mentally, or emotionally. Novelist Nathaniel Hawthorne understood this. He wrote, "A bodily disease, which we look upon as whole and entire within itself, may, after all, be but a symptom of some ailment in the spiritual part."[6]

A good example of this holistic view of body, soul, and spirit is David's psalm following his sin with Bathsheba. Before he was confronted by Nathan about his sin (2 Sam. 12:1–7) and then confessed his sin to the Lord (Ps. 51:1–19), David described the physical pain that came from his unconfessed sin in Psalm 32.

David was likely around fifty years old when he committed adultery with Bathsheba and had her husband, Uriah, murdered, but in Psalm 32, he depicted his physical ailments as if he were a much older man. He wrote, "When I kept silent about my sin, my body wasted away" (v. 3). The word "body" here can be translated as "bones." What David was experiencing spiritually felt like his physical bones being crushed. His spiritual anguish produced physical anguish. No wonder David confessed that he spent his days "groaning" (v. 3)—writhing in pain. "Day and night," he said, God's "hand was heavy upon me" (v. 4), referring to the guilt and shame from his sin. The draining of his spiritual energy resulted in the draining of his physical energy: "My vitality was drained away," he wrote, "as with the fever heat of summer" (v. 4).

An untreated sin-sick spirit can lead to an exhausted body. This often shows up as stress, which can wreak havoc on our bodies. Stress is a leading cause of sleeplessness, stomach ailments, skyrocketing blood pressure, and strokes, just to name a few physical sicknesses resulting from spiritual sickness. Stress causes our bodies to produce cortisol, which, according to one expert, can "open the door to runaway infection, cancer, hyperthyroidism, poor wound healing, diabetes, infertility, and mental instability."[7]

An untreated sin-sick spirit can lead to an exhausted body.

To mask our shame and pain, we tend to go to extremes. We either exercise to the point of exhaustion or become apathetic to the point of being a sluggard; we either sleep so much we become lethargic or sleep so little we become strung out; we either become a workaholic or a slackaholic; we either eat like a bird or eat like a blue whale. A few years ago, a friend lost a good bit of weight during a time when his son was struggling with a serious issue at school. Someone commented on my friend's weight loss. "Stress is a great weight loss program," my friend responded, "if it doesn't kill you first."

There must be a better way to deal with our physical infirmities, whatever the cause. Fortunately, there is. But before we look at those, let's talk about what everybody wants to know: Does the Bible promise health, as some television preachers claim?

Does the Bible Promise Physical Wellness?

There is absolutely no promise in the Bible that exempts Christians from illness and death. Full stop. Nowhere in Scripture does God give us a universal, blanket promise of health and wealth, regardless of what some well-intentioned but misguided believers may tell you.

As I've written in previous chapters, when it comes to praying for a miracle in your life or in the life of a loved one—whether for a miracle of power, provision, protection, or healing—we are all subject to the will and purposes of God in our lives. Even the Son of God was subject to God the Father's will. Jesus told His disciples, "I have come down from heaven, not to do My will, but the will of Him who sent Me" (John 6:38).[8]

When it comes to our own prayers, James encouraged us to use the plainest language possible: "[We] ought to say, '*If the Lord wills*'" (4:15).

Having said that, the Lord is concerned for our physical well-being. He promised the Israelites coming out of Egypt that He would protect them from the diseases He had plagued the Egyptians with. But that promise was conditional. The Israelites had to "give earnest heed to the voice of the LORD your God, and do what is right in His sight, and give ear to His commandments, and keep all His statues" (Exod. 15:26). In the book of Jeremiah, looking toward the coming millennial kingdom, God promised He would "restore [Israel] to health"—to "heal [them] of [their] wounds" (30:17).[9]

But perhaps the best-known verse about the healing providence of God comes from Isaiah 53:5, the great prophecy about the coming Messiah and His death on the cross. Isaiah wrote, "He was pierced through for our transgressions, He was crushed for our iniquities; the chastening for our well-being fell upon Him, and by His scourging we are healed." This verse refers to Jesus's atonement for our sins—our "transgressions" (willful and rebellious acts of sin) and "iniquities" (guilt associated with a sinful soul)—and offers a brutal description of death by crucifixion. Jesus was literally pierced through by being nailed to the cross and having his side sliced open by a Roman lance. And though His legs weren't broken—a common practice to accelerate death—His spirit and body underwent a crushing when the sins of the world were placed upon Him.

Everyone who places faith in Christ will be ultimately healed when we are in the physical presence of the Lord.

Jesus's suffering produces peace and healing for all who place their faith in Him. That's the promise in the last half of the verse: "the chastisement of our peace was upon him; and with his stripes we are healed" (KJV). Because Jesus took the punishment of God's discipline, which was ours to bear, we can experience divine shalom—spiritual, mental, emotional, and physical peace.

Jesus's suffering also brings healing. This is where things get tricky. Some claim this verse teaches universal physical healing for all believers. However, those who teach this have to put qualifiers on it, since their claim flies in the face of reality: Plenty of believers endure any number of physical maladies. To circumvent this reality, bogus teachers and preachers blame those believers who suffer illness or infirmities for not exhibiting enough faith. Nonsense!

The promise of Isaiah 53:5 isn't for universal physical healing for all believers *today*. Rather, it's a promise for universal physical healing for all believers *one day*! Everyone who places faith in Christ will be ultimately healed when we are in the physical presence of the Lord.

Revelation 21:4 gives us this promise: "He will wipe away every tear from their eyes; and there will no longer be any death; there will no longer be any mourning, or crying, or pain; the first things have passed away." That's a promise to cling to!

The Principles of Physical Wellness

God's providential care for our physical health comes in two forms. There are *preventive* actions we should take, as illustrated in the life of Jesus. And there are *prescriptive* actions we should take, as outlined in the book of James.

Preventive Principles

We know very little about Jesus's childhood years. But there's a remarkable verse at the end of Luke's account about the twelve-year-old Jesus who got separated from His parents in Jerusalem during the Passover and was found by them three days later in the temple, conversing with the teachers of the Old Testament (Luke 2:41–46). Luke concluded this story with what seems like a throwaway verse, until we take a closer look: "And Jesus kept increasing in wisdom and stature, and in favor with God and man" (v. 52).

The word translated as "increase" (*prokopto*) means "to move forward to an improved state" of being, to "progress" or "advance."[10] Luke summarized four key areas in Jesus's life where He grew into maturity. We, too, need to develop these areas in our own lives: intellectually ("wisdom"), spiritually ("favor with God"), socially ("favor with . . . man"), and physically ("stature"). We'll leave the first three for another time. Our concern now is with Jesus's physical development and what we can learn from Him, especially when it comes to preventive measures to ensure greater health.

Though we don't have much of a physical description of Jesus (Isa. 53:2), we know He was human and suffered the same frailties we suffer, though without sin. He experienced hunger, thirst, exhaustion, and stress.[11] So, what did He do to "increase" His physical health? He did what we should do.

When Jesus was hungry, He ate. The key word here is *hungry*. He didn't eat to cover up emotional pain or deal with the pressures of life, as many of us do. He ate to satisfy His hunger and to keep His body healthy. What this means for us is simple: We eat when we're hungry, but we don't stuff our faces with cheeseburgers and pizza every day. I don't need to bore you with statistics on the link between good health and healthy food. You know what to do: Eat healthy meals and snacks and increase your intake of fruits and vegetables. It's a question of self-discipline. So, I challenge you to think about your diet for a minute. What's one thing you should cut out or at least cut back on? Do that this week . . . and the next . . . and the next—until it becomes a habit.

When Jesus was thirsty, He drank. Yes, Jesus drank wine, and the apostle Paul told Timothy, "No longer drink water exclusively, but use a little wine for the sake of your stomach and your frequent ailments" (1 Tim. 5:23). But that's not an excuse for alcohol to become our beverage of choice—especially if we want healthy lives. Most of us don't drink nearly enough water, though there are plenty of studies on the benefits of proper hydration. I once heard a guy say, "I don't drink a lot of water, just never saw the purpose in it. In fact, I get most of my daily water intake from several cups of coffee in the morning and a few whiskeys at night."[12] I'm surprised the guy hasn't shriveled up into a ball of dust. How about you? What is the measure of your water intake compared to your intake of alcohol or sugary drinks? Whatever it is, I encourage you to drink more water.

When Jesus was tired, He slept. We don't know how many hours a night Jesus slept, but according to medical experts, the average adult needs seven or more hours of sleep a night.[13] So, how much sleep do you get every night? If it's less than seven hours, and especially if you're feeling tired, then perhaps you need to hit the sack a little earlier or break the habit of looking at your phone just before bed. Read a book instead. Or better yet, tuck yourself in and have a conversation with the Lord.

When Jesus was under pressure, He retreated. Throughout the Gospels, we see Jesus finding a quiet place by Himself to spend time with the Father.[14] This is a good practice for anyone dealing with stress. Get off social media. Turn off the news. Read a book. Go for a walk. Develop a hobby. Pet a dog or a cat. Exercise regularly. Spend more time with God, as Jesus did. What can you do to take care of your physical health when pressure comes?

Prescriptive Principles

Of course, we might do all the above, but we will eventually contract an illness or disease. Why do Christians get sick? The short answer is that we inhabit bodies that have an expiration date on them. The bodies we inhabit in this fallen world were never designed to last forever. Beyond that general truth, the Bible gives three specific categories of illness.

First, there is a *sickness leading to death*, as referred to in John 11:4 and Philippians 2:27. Simply put, if we never got sick, we would never die—which may *sound* good but ultimately would be tragic. Death is a necessary experience to transition us from this world to the wonderful future God has for every Christian. This is one reason

I don't generally get too excited over stories of physical healing. As miraculous as any physical healing may be, it's only temporary. Eventually, every healed person will get sick again and will die—and that's a good thing!

As miraculous as any physical healing may be, it's only temporary.

Second, some *sickness is a result of personal sin.* That sin could include the natural consequences of not taking care of our bodies because of gluttony, alcohol or drug abuse, or some other harmful lifestyle choice. Other times, the sin causing our illness may be a direct judgment from God, as Miriam experienced in Numbers 12 because of her disobedience to God.

Finally, some *sickness is for the glory of God.* Sometimes God is exalted through a miraculous healing, such as the blind man whom Jesus healed in John 9 that proved Jesus was the long-awaited Messiah. Jesus said about this man's physical blindness, "It was neither that this man sinned, nor his parents; but it was so that the works of God might be displayed in him" (v. 3). Think about this: The entire reason this man suffered a lifetime of blindness until the day he encountered Jesus was so that people would know that Jesus is the Savior of the world!

But other times, God is glorified through our *lack* of healing from our illness. In 2 Corinthians 12, the apostle Paul recounted how he had pleaded with God on three different occasions to remove his "thorn in the flesh" (v. 7), which most commentators identify as some physical malady. Yet God answered no each time Paul asked for healing. Paul concluded, "And He has said to me, 'My grace is sufficient for you, for power is perfected in weakness.' Most gladly, therefore, I will rather boast about my weaknesses, so that the power of Christ may dwell in me" (v. 9). God's power is most clearly seen in our weakness, not in our strength.

Every time I think about that truth, I picture my friend Joni Eareckson Tada. When Joni was seventeen, a diving accident left her confined to a wheelchair—for over six decades so far. In an op-ed piece a few years ago, Joni recounted how she prayed and visited faith healers in search of a miracle for the first years after her accident. But she ultimately came to this conclusion:

> Does God miraculously heal? Sure, he does. But in this broken world, it's still the exception, not the rule. A "no" answer to my request for a miraculous physical healing has meant purged sin, a love for the lost, increased compassion, stretched hope, an appetite for grace, an increase of faith, a happy longing for heaven, a desire to serve, a delight in prayer, and a hunger for his Word. Oh, bless the stern schoolmaster that is my wheelchair![15]

So, what should we do when we become ill? James, the half brother of Jesus, gives us a prescription for handling illnesses that invade our lives: "Is any among you sick? Then he must call for the elders of the church and they are to pray over him, anointing him with oil in the name of the Lord; and the prayer offered in faith will restore the one who is sick, and the Lord will raise him up, and if he has committed sins, they will be forgiven him" (James 5:14–15).

First, when you are sick, *go to the doctor*. You may be asking, "Where do you find doctors and medicine in this passage from James 5?" The Greek text of verse 14 actually says, "having anointed him with oil, let them pray." Oil was a medicinal agent in the first century. For example, the good Samaritan used oil as a healing agent for the man ambushed by robbers (Luke 10:34).

When you are sick, seek the best medicines and the best doctors available. After all, even Jesus acknowledged the need for physicians.

In Isaiah 38, we read the story of King Hezekiah's illness that seemed terminal. Yet Hezekiah prayed that God would heal him and lengthen his life. God miraculously answered the king's prayer, but look at *how* He answered it: "Now Isaiah had said, 'Let them take a cake of figs and apply it to the boil, that he may recover'" (v. 21). God didn't need figs to heal Hezekiah, but He was teaching a truth to all generations: When you are sick, seek the best medicines and the best doctors available. After all, even Jesus acknowledged the need for physicians when He said, "It is not those who are healthy who need a physician, but those who are sick" (Matt. 9:12).

When you are sick, *don't forget to pray*—and have others pray for you as well. Notice that I didn't begin the previous sentence with "second," as if prayer were secondary to doctors and medicine. Just as James implied, while we are seeking medical help ("the oil"), we are also to pray for healing and have others pray for us as well, especially spiritual leaders ("the elders").

At First Baptist Church in Dallas, we don't have "faith healing" services, but we regularly have what I call "faith-kneeling" services, in which I invite people who need physical, emotional, or spiritual healing to come to the altar and pray with one of the leaders of the church. If they have sins in their lives that may be the cause of their illness, they can ask Christ to forgive them.

People flood the aisles for the possibility of having a godly leader interceding on their behalf for healing and restoration. They believe James's assurance that "the effective prayer of a righteous man can accomplish much" (James 5:16).

I'm always careful to explain before we begin the prayer time that there is no guarantee that praying will result in physical healing. As we have seen in this chapter, there are times God says no to our request. But sometimes He answers yes.

Sometimes we are led to believe by misinformed Christians that our failure to experience miraculous healing is the result of our lack of faith. After all, didn't James say that "the prayer offered in faith will restore the one who is sick" (v. 15)?

Let's be clear about what true, biblical faith is and what it is not. Faith is *not* the assurance that God will do what we want Him to do. Faith is the assurance that God will do what is best for us. When it comes to praying for healing, faith is boldly asking God to do what we want and quietly trusting in Him to do what is best. As Jesus prayed in the garden of Gethsemane before He was crucified, "My Father, if it is possible, let this cup pass from Me; yet not as I will, but as You will" (Matt. 26:39).

Finally, whenever we confront illness in our lives or in the life of someone we love, we should *always seek to glorify God*. Many years ago, I went to visit a couple in my church with a son who had been severely ill. They had spent years wondering why God allowed their son to be ill and refused to answer their request for healing.

When it comes to praying for healing, faith is boldly asking God to do what we want and quietly trusting in Him to do what is best.

One night, both parents were awakened at 2 a.m. and felt led to pray for God's intervention in their situation. They were terribly discouraged and running out of money. Later that morning, while they were in the hospital waiting room before they went in to see their son, a man approached them and said, "I don't mean to offend you, but may I ask you a personal question? How are your finances holding up?"

The wife told the truth about their situation, and the man pulled out a wad of $100 bills and handed it to the couple. He explained, "The Lord awakened me at 2 a.m. and told me to give this money to someone I would meet today." It turned out that the man was a multimillionaire, and along with the cash, he also gave them his private phone number. He told the boy's parents, "If you need more money, just call me. I am a tool of the Holy Spirit, and this is the ministry God has given me!"

After relating that story to me, the mother said, "That was the first time in the sixty years of my life that I had ever seen the hand of God."

She and her family were given a new zeal for God. Because of a stack of $100 bills? No. Because they had seen the power of God displayed through sickness, not healing.

The longer I live, the more convinced I am that God is much more interested in the renewed spiritual commitment of that entire family than in the temporary affliction—or the temporary healing—of their son. We serve an all-powerful God who continues to perform miracles, sometimes through healing and sometimes through sickness.

CHAPTER 6

WHEN YOUR MIRACLE DOESN'T COME

BEFORE DOUGLAS GROOTHUIS earned the distinguished title Doctor of Philosophy, he was a campus minister at the University of Oregon. It was there that he met Rebecca, an intelligent writer and editor. They married a year later.

Doug has written many books, but Rebecca was the real wordsmith. "She loved language," Doug told Lee Strobel in an interview. "She could write magnificent sentences that flowed for sixty words or more."[1] Doug teaches apologetics at Denver Seminary, but Rebecca was the real intellectual—a member of Mensa.

About a year into their marriage, Rebecca was diagnosed with fibromyalgia, a disorder that affects the way pain signals are processed in the nervous system. In what some call "fibro fog," Rebecca began forgetting things, like how to find her way back home after her appointment at the hair salon. Doug had to file a missing person's report with the police. Another time, she couldn't remember how to start her car or how to turn on the windshield wipers. Doctors offered no answers.

Then, in 2014, Doug rushed Rebecca to the hospital. "She couldn't . . . get out of bed. She couldn't talk," Doug told Strobel. Emergency room doctors found nothing physically wrong, though she exhibited depression-like symptoms, so they called in a psychiatrist, who eventually admitted her to a psychiatric hospital. "They strapped her down and took her away on a stretcher—she looked so forlorn," Doug said.

She was there for five weeks and was diagnosed with primary progressive aphasia, a rare neurological disorder that attacks portions of the brain that control the ability to speak and write. As Doug explained, "It begins in the frontal lobe of the brain and moves backward, which is the opposite of Alzheimer's. You lose your use of words and then your executive functions—the ability to analyze and perform tasks. The particular cruelty of this disease is that you slowly lose your mind—and you're aware of it slipping away."

Doug and Rebecca lived with the slow, creeping diminishment of her cognitive abilities for four years. Through it all, they and others prayed for God to intervene, beseeching Him for healing. The Lord said no.

"I didn't know a soul could endure so much emotional anguish," Doug said. "I'm becoming an expert on suffering." In 2017, a year before Rebecca's death, Doug wrote about the emotional and spiritual toll her illness took on him and how he wrestled with God's decision not to heal her. In *Walking Through Twilight*, Doug concluded:

> "Love is as strong as death" (Song of Songs 8:6), and stronger. We know this because of an innocent man nailed to a Roman pike of shame, festooned by a dying criminal on each side. That young man died and was buried. Three days later, his tomb was emptied of death and he was found more alive than any of us are right now. These

> matchless and unmatchable events—written in books, but resident in reality—are my only hope in life and death, in Becky's life and in Becky's death. Jesus is Lord.[2]

Jesus is Lord. That is the only hope for those who've pleaded with God for a miracle, only to find the answer coming back a resounding no.

Does this describe your situation? Have you needed a miracle, and it didn't come? Have you poured out your heart to God only to have your request returned empty?

There's a danger in unanswered prayer. You can easily conclude God has turned a deaf ear to your pleas or believe He's too busy to bother with your problems. Worse still, you might conclude God no longer loves you—if He ever did. None of this is true, of course, and you probably know that in your head. But your heart struggles to understand why God wouldn't answer your prayer, especially if it was for a loved one. Like a gut punch, your unanswered prayer is a blow to your faith.

Jesus is Lord. That is the only hope for those who've pleaded with God for a miracle, only to find the answer coming back a resounding no.

The writer to the Hebrews defined faith as "the assurance of things hoped for, the conviction of things not seen" (11:1). John Wesley paraphrased this verse like this: "Faith is the power to see into the world of spirits, into things invisible and eternal. It is the power to understand those things which are not perceived by worldly senses."[3]

To see what is unseen, we must develop a sixth sense—a spiritual sense, particularly during times of suffering. This only comes through faith—believing that God is who He says He is and that He can and will do what He says He will do. Oswald Chambers writes, "Faith is deliberate confidence in the character of God Whose ways you cannot understand in time. . . . I don't know why God allows what He does, but I will stick to my faith in His character no matter how contradictory things look."[4]

To strengthen your belief in God's goodness, power, and sovereignty—to help you develop that sixth sense—I encourage you to put into practice the following five principles.

Principle #1: Rest in God's Grace

There are any number of reasons God might not answer our prayers, including our prayers for a miracle. The Bible gives us at least seven:

1. Not praying from a pure heart (Ps. 66:18).
2. Not praying in faith (James 1:5–8).
3. Not praying from an obedient life (1 John 3:22).
4. Not praying to bring glory to God (1 Cor. 10:31).
5. Not praying with a goal toward sanctification (1 Thess. 4:3).
6. Not praying with an attitude of humility (Luke 18:9–14).
7. Not praying in conjunction with the Holy Spirit (Eph. 6:18).[5]

In addition to this list, the Lord might choose to say no to your prayers for other reasons. For example, the apostle Paul hadn't violated anything on this list, yet when he asked the Lord three times to remove his "thorn in the flesh, a messenger of Satan to torment me" (2 Cor. 12:7), God said no. "My grace is sufficient for you," the Lord said, "for power is perfected in weakness" (v. 9).[6]

Paul prayed for alleviation; God gave him alteration—a new perspective on his pain: grace. This might be the case for you. The Lord may be saying, "No. No. No." If that's the case, rest in the fact that His no is always accompanied by His grace.

It's been said that in His mercy, God doesn't give us what we *do deserve*, and, in His grace, God gives us what we *don't deserve*. Grace is God's provision to meet your needs when you need it—"grace upon grace," as the apostle John put it (John 1:16). Just as the Lord did with Paul, so He might be using your weakness as a demonstration of His *sufficient grace* and His *strengthening grace*.

He might be using your weakness as a demonstration of His sufficient grace and His strengthening grace.

British preacher Charles Spurgeon wrote, "I venture to say that the greatest earthly blessing that God can give to any of us is health, with the exception of sickness. Sickness has frequently been of more use to the saints of God than health."[7] It's true—if we rest in God's grace, allowing it to work in us and through us.

How do we do that? By spending time in God's Word, which Acts 20:32 calls "the word of His grace." In it, we will find the Lord's sufficient and strengthening grace, just as He promised. Warren Wiersbe said it well: "*We do not live on explanations; we live on promises.* Our feelings change, but God's promises never change."[8]

One of the graces of God, when we commit ourselves to daily Bible reading, is growth in faith and hope. As Wiersbe wrote, "Promises generate faith, and faith strengthens hope."[9] Our intake of Scripture—or lack thereof—is directly linked to the strength of our faith. Commenting on the details of Jesus's life and ministry, John wrote, "These have been written so that you may believe that Jesus is the Christ, the Son of God; and that believing you may have life in His name" (John 20:31). Paul said something similar in Romans 10:17: "So faith comes from hearing, and hearing by the word of Christ."

Evangelist George Müller understood the connection between faith and the Bible. He wrote, "Faith has to do with the word of God—[it] rests upon the written word of God."[10] What we think is possible or impossible has nothing to do with our faith. The only important question is what God has said in His Word.

When life becomes stressful, especially when your hoped-for and prayed-for miracle doesn't come, don't look for a way of escape or turn your back on the Lord for His failure to deliver what you want; instead, dive deeper into God's Word. Saturate your mind and heart with His Word, and you'll find the grace and faith to go on.

Principle #2: Learn to Wait for God's Timing

The Lord sometimes tests our faith before He answers our prayers. A dramatic illustration of this is found in the book of Exodus.

After God delivered the Israelites from Egypt and began guiding them on their journey to the promised land, He led them to a place called Marah—a name that means "bitter." It was a place where they had to trust God to transform undrinkable water into drinkable water (Exod. 15:22–23). On their way to the promised land, the Lord could have bypassed Marah and led them straight to the oasis of Elim, where there was an abundance of clean, refreshing water (v. 27). But He didn't.

At Marah, "the people grumbled at Moses, saying, 'What shall we drink?'" (v. 24). They would have gone thirsty if Moses hadn't intervened: "Then he cried out to the Lord, and the Lord showed him a tree; and he threw it into the waters, and the waters became sweet" (v. 25). Moses then added, "There [God] made for them a statute and regulation, and there He tested them. And He said, 'If you will give earnest heed to the voice of the Lord your God, and do what is right in His sight, and give ear to His commandments, and keep all His statutes, I will put none of the diseases on you which I have put on the Egyptians; for I, the Lord, am your healer'" (vv. 25–26).

The Lord sometimes tests our faith before He answers our prayers.

The Lord does something similar in our lives. Before delivering on a needed divine intervention in our lives, He might stretch our faith by causing us to wait or by bringing a challenging circumstance into our lives to see whether we'll grumble in disbelief, as the Israelites did, or continue to pray in faith and rest in His grace. It's a test of endurance.

James pointed out, "The testing of your faith produces *endurance*. And let *endurance* have its perfect result, so that you may be perfect and complete, lacking in nothing" (1:3–4). The endurance James was talking about is the ability to stand on your feet during a storm. It's spiritual fortitude and toughness. It's learning to become a spiritual Rocky Balboa—to take punch after punch without hitting the mat.

I endured such a test of faith when the Lord led me from the church I served as pastor in Eastland, Texas, to another ministry. I received a call from a large church in Virginia, wanting me to serve as their senior pastor. Amy and I were excited about the possibility. The church was growing and had a large television ministry, something I desired to be involved in.

We pulled out all the stops for the search committee's visit. We planted fresh flowers in front of the parsonage and the sanctuary and made sure the church was spick-and-span, and I selected my best sermon to preach that Sunday. After the service, the search committee from this large church wanted to set a date for me to come and preach to their congregation in view of an official invitation to become their senior pastor.

This was the first test. I believed the Lord was in the process of moving Amy and me from Eastland, and the Virginia opportunity had everything I longed for in ministry. But I had made a commitment to the Lord and to myself never to accept a call to pastor without first visiting and speaking with the congregants and getting a sense from staff members what the Lord was doing there. I suggested to the search committee members that we set a date for Amy and me to visit the church before setting a date for me to preach there. They agreed and said they would talk it over with the full committee and get back to me later that week.

This was the second test. Amy and I had all but packed our bags, thinking we'd receive a call on Monday or Tuesday at the latest. Monday came and went. No big deal. It was wishful thinking that the full committee would meet on Monday and call before the end of the day. On Tuesday morning, I woke with anticipation. All day I checked my watch as the hours ticked away—and I stared at the telephone. When I turned off the lights in my office at the end of the day, I hadn't heard a peep from the large church. Wednesday was torture—and it came and went in silence.

What were these people doing? What was the Lord doing? Then Thursday came. My phone rang and my heart leaped. I hate to admit it, but my heart sank just as quickly when the voice on the other end said, "Hello." It was a friend, not a member of the Virginia church's search committee. What my friend said next served as concrete shoes for my spirit. He knew of the ministry opportunity and said he had reliable information that the church was considering another pastor. I was heartbroken.

The following Monday, while I was getting my hair cut, my cell phone rang. It was a man I'd never heard of. "This is Harold Warren," he said. "I'm the chair of the pastoral search committee at First Baptist Church in Wichita Falls, Texas. We'd like to talk with you about the possibility of you serving as our pastor." I was still reeling from the disappointment of the previous week, so I said nonchalantly, "When would you like to come and hear me preach?" Harold said, "We don't need to do that. We've been in your service three times, including last Sunday, and we're ready to talk with you about becoming our pastor."

I asked him when they wanted to come and talk. He said, "This afternoon." The committee members piled into a van and drove two and a half hours from Wichita Falls to Eastland. Amy and I spent the evening with them discussing the possibility and set a date for us to visit their church, which we did that weekend.

When we returned home and walked through the door, our phone was ringing. I answered it. The man introduced himself as a search committee member from the Virginia church and asked, "Where have you been? We've been trying to reach you all weekend."

I explained that another church was interested in me, I had been with them over the weekend, and I had accepted their offer to become their senior pastor. "No, no, that's not God's will," the man on the phone said. "It's God's will for you to come to our church." I told him I was under the impression that his search committee was interested in another pastor. "No," he said. "There was one committee member who wanted to check out another candidate, but we're unanimous that we want you, Robert."

This was the third test. Though I had given my word to pastor in Wichita Falls, the Virginia opportunity seemed too good to pass up. The door I thought had closed was now wide open. But I said to the man on the phone, "I'm sorry. I've accepted the call to Wichita Falls."

I've never regretted that decision. What happened in our church in Wichita Falls over the next fifteen years was more than anything I could have ever dreamed of! The Lord used the fifteen years in Wichita Falls to mature me and prepare me for an even greater ministry with a global impact.

That experience taught me an unforgettable lesson about miracles that don't come. If we endure in our faith—being obedient to follow God in every decision we make—God sometimes replaces what could have been a miracle with an even greater miracle!

Principle #3: Adjust Your Attitude

Chuck Swindoll famously wrote, "The longer I live the more convinced I become that life is 10 percent what happens to us and 90 percent how we respond to it."[11] When our miracle doesn't come, we need to abandon the attitude of self-pity and bitterness and adopt the attitude of joy—the inner peace found in resting in God's grace.

When James taught about endurance in the verses we looked at earlier, he prefaced his message about endurance with these words: "*Consider it all joy*, my brethren, when you encounter various trials" (1:2). Now, he didn't mean we should rejoice because we're facing trials. Nor is he suggesting a white-knuckle approach to difficulties that says, "Just grin and bear it!" No. James meant that we should make a conscious and careful decision to maintain an attitude of joy even during times of trouble. The Greek word translated as "consider" (*hegeomai*) means "to lead" or "to guide." James 1:2 instructs us to make joy our leading thought whenever we experience some difficulty or disappointment.

I know what you're thinking: *Yeah, right! That's just a bunch of pie-in-the-sky thinking to make me feel better about my job loss, the cancer diagnosis I just received, or the divorce I just went through. And God was nowhere to be found.* I understand. A fellow pastor struggled with many of the same thoughts when his wife underwent five major surgeries for cancer, including bouts of radiation and chemotherapy, while at the same time, several staff members resigned and left his church. But he chose joy and found his spirit lifted from the doldrums. He wrote,

> The greatest discovery that I have made in the midst of all the difficulties is that I can have joy when I can't feel like it—artesian joy. When I had every reason to feel beaten, I felt joy. In spite of everything, [God] gave me the conviction of being loved and the certainty that nothing could separate me from him. It was not happiness, gush, or jolliness but a constant flow of the Spirit through me. At

> no time did he give me the easy confidence that everything could work out as I wanted it on my timetable, but that he was in charge and would give me and my family enough courage for each day: grace. Joy is always the result of that.[12]

With the proper attitude, bitterness is taken out of even the severest trials and replaced with the sweetness of joy.

Adjust your attitude. Choose joy.

Principle #4: Maintain Your Perspective

British journalist Richard Hamilton recounted a story from Morocco that helps put things into perspective:

> A king was whittling a piece of wood one day and accidentally sliced off part of his finger. His optimistic prime minister said, "It's good." Stinging from the cut and the remark, and in a fit of anger, the king put the prime minister in prison. A few days later, with his finger bandaged, the king took a vacation on one of his ships.
>
> When he arrived at a beautiful island and disembarked by himself, he was attacked by natives who intended to sacrifice him. But when the high priest noticed a part of the king's finger was missing the high priest released him as an unsuitable sacrifice.
>
> The king arrived back in his kingdom and freed his prime minister and told him what had happened on the island. The king then asked: "How was your time in jail?"
>
> The prime minister said, "It's good."
>
> "How could it be good?"

"Well," the prime minister said, "if you'd taken me to the island, you would have escaped but I would have been sacrificed."[13]

Suffering has a way of sharpening our perspective—of clarifying and bringing into focus what is good and what is bad, what is necessary and what is superfluous, what is holy and what is unholy. When we ask God for a miracle and He says no, we must maintain our perspective on two essentials.

First, we *keep our eyes on Christ* and never let our desire for a miracle come between us and Jesus. The object of our faith is Christ, not miracles. As Bible teacher Adrian Rogers put it, we must "learn to believe in miracles, but to trust in Jesus."[14] The writer to the Hebrews said of our life of faith, "Let us run with endurance the race that is set before us, fixing our eyes on Jesus, the author and perfecter of faith, who for the joy set before Him, endured the cross, despising the shame, and has sat down at the right hand of the throne of God. For consider Him who has endured such hostility by sinners against Himself, so that you will not grow weary and lose heart" (12:1–3).

Suffering has a way of sharpening our perspective.

I'm often asked why God allows a financial difficulty, a rebellious child, or an incurable disease—and why He hasn't intervened. God rarely answers the "why" question. Rather, He gives us Christ as an example to follow, to encourage us to move forward in faith. In 2 Corinthians

4:17–18, Paul, a man well-versed in suffering, wrote, "For momentary, light affliction is producing for us an eternal weight of glory far beyond all comparison, while we look not at the things which are seen, but at the things which are not seen; for the things which are seen are temporal, but the things which are not seen are eternal."

Paul was saying that whatever we're suffering through right now, along with our disappointment with God, is "momentary" and "light." Paul didn't diminish the reality of suffering, but he asked us to keep it in perspective when it comes to the length and intensity of our trials.

You may have been waiting for years or even decades for your miracle. But that waiting is "momentary" compared to eternity. How long is eternity? Someone once described eternity as being like a bird coming to Mount Everest to sharpen its beak once every million years. By the time the bird succeeds in wearing the mountain down to a pebble, the clock on eternity wouldn't have ticked one second. It's a matter of perspective.

Or think about the intensity of the pain of your trial. Paul said it is "light." It's easy to say, "Well, Paul didn't know what I've been through." Yes, he did. Paul was rejected by friends, imprisoned, beaten, and ultimately beheaded, but he said those were "light afflictions" compared to the blessings he would experience in heaven.

Think of a two-ton boulder: Is it "light" or "heavy"? Compared to a 787 jetliner, it is light; compared to a feather, it is heavy. No matter how heavy the burden is that you are carrying, it is light in comparison to the joy you will experience in heaven one day. In eternity, miracles will no longer be needed. God has promised to "wipe away every tear" because there "will no longer be any death; there will no longer be any mourning, or crying, or pain; the first things have passed away" (Rev. 21:4).

Keeping your eyes on Christ by "[setting] your mind on the things above, not on the things that are on earth" (Col. 3:2) won't eliminate the disappointments, diseases, and death of this world, but it will put your pain in perspective.

Second, we *remember that God is working all things for our good.* When it came to suffering and the disappointment of unanswered prayers, Paul was no Pollyanna. Before he was beheaded in Rome, Paul suffered imprisonments, a shipwreck, five life-threatening beatings, and a painful malady—all in the name of Christ. Yet he not only boasted in his weakness because of God's grace (2 Cor. 12:9–10) but also penned one of the most beloved verses in the New Testament: "We know that God causes all things to work together for good to those who love God, to those who are called according to His purpose" (Rom. 8:28). The "good" Paul had in mind here is spiritual maturity, just as he said in verse 29: "For those whom He foreknew, He also predestined to become conformed to the image of His Son, so that He would be the firstborn among many brethren."

No matter how heavy the burden is that you are carrying, it is light in comparison to the joy you will experience in heaven one day.

Like sailors at sea who lose sight of land, it's easy to lose sight of Christ and how we're being molded into His image. This is especially true when the Lord refuses to bring relief, when the miracle we've prayed for doesn't come. Most people only see the shore once they've passed through the pain.

This was true of Soviet dissident Aleksandr Solzhenitsyn. During World War II, because he was critical of Joseph Stalin, Solzhenitsyn was thrown into a Soviet gulag, where he came to faith in Christ. Years later, while writing a history of the Soviet prison system, Solzhenitsyn expressed his gratitude for the years he spent there.

> It was granted me to carry away from my prison years on my bent back, which nearly broke beneath its load, this essential experience: *how* a human being becomes evil and *how* good. . . . It was only when I lay there on rotting prison straw that I sensed within myself the first stirrings of good. . . . And that is why I turn back to the years of my imprisonment and say, sometimes to the astonishment of those about me: "*Bless you prison!*" . . . All the writers who wrote about prison but who did not themselves serve time there considered it their duty to express sympathy for prisoners and to curse prison. I . . . have served enough time there. I nourished my soul there, and I say without hesitation: "*Bless you prison*, for having been in my life!"[15]

Solzhenitsyn didn't want to suffer, but like Job, he could say, "The Lord gave and the Lord has taken away. Blessed be the name of the Lord" (Job 1:21).

I'm guessing you don't want to suffer either. You desire your longed-for miracle. But if your miracle doesn't come, you can rest assured it doesn't mean God has forgotten about you or doesn't love you. It may mean God has a purpose for your suffering that you can't yet see. Or perhaps God may be using your suffering for something better. Your life doesn't consist of avoiding suffering but of turning your suffering into something good. A mother endures the pain of childbirth because she knows her suffering leads to something glorious—new life.

For Job, the apostle Paul, and Solzhenitsyn, suffering had a deep meaning. Each matured spiritually because of his suffering, making it easier to endure that suffering. If you can wrap your head around the truth that God is working everything out for your good and His glory, then you can transform your suffering into praise.

Principle #5: Develop a Ministry-Focused Life

As a pastor, I talk to a lot of people who are disappointed with God for His failure to answer their prayers in the ways they want. These are folks who didn't receive a cure for the disease that eventually took the life of their loved one, or didn't find renewed love with a spouse who eventually divorced them, or didn't see their prodigal child return to the faith. Whenever I speak to one of these hurting believers, I encourage them with the words of 2 Corinthians 1:3–4: "Blessed be the God and Father of our Lord Jesus Christ, the Father of mercies and God of all comfort, who comforts us in all our affliction so that we will be able to comfort those who are in any affliction with the comfort with which we ourselves are comforted by God."

God the Father is characterized by mercy, and He is the source of all the mercies we've ever experienced in life. As the Father of mercies, even if God doesn't grant our specific prayer for a miracle, He shows Himself also to be the Father of comfort. This doesn't simply mean that He feels sympathy for our suffering but that He actively saddles up alongside each of us to encourage and support us during our days of difficulty. The Greek word translated as "comfort" actually means "to strengthen."

The Father strengthens us through His Son, Jesus, who serves as our Advocate before the Father (1 John 2:1) and our Helper during times of distress (Heb. 2:18). The Father also consoles us through His Holy Spirit, who guides and strengthens us.[16]

The Father's strength comes to us not only through the Son and the Spirit but also through the saints—fellow believers who come near to minister to us. Often, brothers and sisters in Christ can intervene in our lives when we are suffering and help us endure an affliction.

However, the real key to 2 Corinthians 1:3–4 is not that we find comfort in the Son, the Spirit, and the saints ourselves but that *we comfort (strengthen) others*. Every time somebody speaks to me about their troubles, not only do I try to offer biblical advice and encourage them with God's comfort but I also tell them that a day will come when they'll have an opportunity to minister to someone who's dealing with the same struggle.

For example, I can offer marriage counseling, but since Amy and I have a strong marriage, I can only empathize so much with a couple on the verge of divorce. But someone who has endured a divorce and come out the other side healthy can. I can weep with a couple who've lost a child to cancer, but I can't fully enter their grief and walk them through the emotional and spiritual land mines that lie ahead because I haven't lost a child. But someone who has survived the loss of a child and kept their faith intact can.

Reach out to help another person who's praying for a miracle. Perhaps you are God's answer to their prayer.

There are a thousand other examples: financial devastation, a prodigal child, drug addiction, pornography addiction, mental illness, depression, anxiety, physical disability—and the list goes on. I may not have experienced these specific hardships, and though I can offer the best I can in biblical counsel and consolation, at some point I tap out because I've not walked those paths. But you might have. And if you have, then reach out to help another person who's praying for a miracle. Perhaps you are God's answer to their prayer.

As we wrap up this chapter, let me be painfully blunt: God has not promised a miracle for everyone, every time, to meet our every need. In the list of faithful followers found in Hebrews 11, the writer concludes by describing Old Testament saints who didn't see God's miraculous intervention in saving them from suffering.

Yet these godly men and women are highly honored for their continued faith.

> They were stoned, they were sawn in two, they were tempted, they were put to death with the sword; they went about in sheepskins, in goatskins, being destitute, afflicted, ill-treated (men of whom the world was not worthy), wandering in deserts and mountains and caves and holes in the ground.
>
> And all these, having gained approval through their faith, did not receive what was promised, *because God had provided something better for us*. (Heb. 11:37–40)

That "something better" is Jesus Christ and all His promises that the Old Testament saints longed to experience. God didn't deny those saints that ultimate promise; He just delayed it for a future time.

And so it is with us. Miracles delayed aren't miracles denied. One day when we are united with Jesus Christ in heaven, we will experience the fulfillment of every miracle we have ever longed for.

CHAPTER 7

BEWARE OF COUNTERFEIT MIRACLES

I WAS RECENTLY TALKING with a friend who ministers at another church. He told me about a woman who started attending the adult fellowship he taught. Her husband, a successful businessman, wasn't interested in spiritual matters, so he never came with her. Her two college-age children were away at school, so she attended alone. One day, she called my friend in a panic. Her son had been found dead in his fraternity house. He and his fraternity brothers had a pledge party, and he passed out drunk on a couch. When the party was over, the rest of the fraternity members went to bed. The next morning, they found him on the floor unresponsive, cold, and blue. The toxicology report said he died of alcohol poisoning.

She called my friend because she didn't know who else to call at the church. He notified the ministerial staff to help the family during their time of grief. My friend met with the family, as did the senior pastor, to offer comfort and assist with funeral arrangements. The boy's mother told my friend and the senior pastor that her son was a Christian. They assured her that if that was the case, then he was in the presence of the Lord, just as 2 Corinthians 5:8 promises.

Yet she believed in the notion that while her son's physical body had ceased to function, his spirit hadn't gone to heaven but was present with her. She said others had told her that the spirits of dearly loved ones didn't depart at death but instead lingered to comfort the grieving and stayed until the grieving were ready to let them go. She said these counselors advised her to look for manifestations of her son's presence because he would visit her to mend her broken heart.

They assured her that he would appear as an apparition of light. She became convinced this was true and held on to it like a lifeline, no matter what Scripture teaches about the spirits of deceased believers being in the presence of Christ. She told my friend and the senior pastor that she believed her son appeared to her every morning in the breakfast nook of the family home where she drank her coffee. She claimed that he materialized in the morning rays of light as they passed through the limbs of the trees—his face reflected against the wall and hovered above the chair where he used to sit eating his breakfast and drinking his own coffee.

She couldn't deny the reality of her son's physical death. She had seen his body. But in her grief, she couldn't accept the reality that her son's spirit would leave her. He just wouldn't do that. Nothing my friend or the senior pastor said from God's Word could convince her that what she saw in the morning light was only her imagination. So, she listened to charlatans who tickled her ears with lies.

When my friend told me this story, I thought of the apostle Paul's warning in 2 Corinthians 11:14–15: "Satan . . . masquerades as an angel of light. It is not surprising, then, if his servants also masquerade themselves as servants of righteousness" (NIV). To deceive others, Satan, who is full of darkness and death, must put on a mask of light and life, but it's a lie "because there is no truth in him," as Jesus said. "Whenever he speaks a lie, he speaks from his own nature, for he is a liar and the father of lies" (John 8:44).

Those who tell grieving parents that the spirit of their dead loved one will visit them as an apparition of light are also lying, deceiving others by disguising and denying the truth. Don't listen to such people. And don't be taken in by faux phenomena such as apparitions being passed off as genuine works of God.

I understand this is easier said than done, but the following warnings, if heeded, will keep you from being duped into believing lies from the evil one.

Satan's Temporary Power over This World

The Bible is clear that "our struggle is not against flesh and blood, but against the rulers, against the powers, against the world forces of this darkness, against the spiritual forces of wickedness in the heavenly places" where Satan rules (Eph. 6:12). To avoid falling for deceptive "signs and false wonders" (2 Thess. 2:9), we must first understand how the father of lies operates.

Satan is portrayed in Scripture as extremely powerful and influential. He's called "the ruler of this world" (John 12:31), "the god of this world" (2 Cor. 4:4), and the "prince of the power of the air" (Eph. 2:2). He exerts power over humans, governments, angels, and religion.[1]

Though the devil's power is great, it's not as great as God's power. For example, Satan can only be in one place at a time, while God is *omnipresent*—present in all places at all times. Satan can only know so much, while God is *omniscient*—all-knowing. Satan can exercise only so much power, while God is *omnipotent*—all-powerful. So, although Satan is described as a roaring lion prowling around looking for his next meal (1 Pet. 5:8), he's a lion on a leash—and God holds the other end of that leash and determines its length.

There's an old proverb that uses another creature to describe Satan. It says, "The Devil is the ape of God," referring to the act of mimicking God.[2] How does Satan "ape" God?

- Satan has established his own *throne* to inspire his own *worshipers* (Rev. 13:2, 4), *church*—the "synagogue of Satan" (Rev. 2:9), and *theological system*—called "doctrines of demons" (1 Tim. 4:1; see also Rev. 2:24).
- He supports his own *ministers*—priests of darkness who preach false messages (2 Cor. 11:4–5). These consist of *false teachers* who bring "destructive heresies" (2 Pet. 2:1) and *false prophets* and *false apostles* who pass themselves off as true prophets and apostles (Matt. 24:11; 2 Cor. 11:13).
- All of these false teachers preach a *false gospel*—one contrary to the "gospel . . . [the true apostles] have preached" (Gal. 1:7–8).[3]

It's all smoke and mirrors, meant to deceive us from what is true. Satan is like General George Patton during World War II, just before the invasion of Normandy. Patton commanded the First US Army Group, better known as the Ghost Army, and was stationed outside of Dover, England, opposite Calais, France. The English Channel funnels into its narrowest neck between these two towns, making Calais the obvious place for the Allies to invade Europe in 1944. To convince the Germans that's exactly what the Allies planned to do, they made it known that Patton was commanding a vast army in the vicinity of Dover, and they stationed rubber decoys—tanks, trucks, and airplanes—around the village while the real invasion plans called for landing at Normandy. The deception worked.

Satan employs a similar strategy today, convincing us to prepare for a spiritual attack over here while he attacks over there. He's a master magician, performing sleights of hand to persuade us that his "counterfeit power and signs and miracles" (2 Thess. 2:9 NLT) are the real deal.

As we saw in the first chapter, a man named Simon, mentioned in the book of Acts, was one of Satan's servants who tried to pass himself off as one of the "servants of righteousness" (2 Cor. 11:15). But he wasn't performing legitimate miracles. He was "practicing magic" or sorcery (Acts 8:9) to deceive the people of Samaria into praising him as "the Great Power of God" (v. 10).

But when it comes to counterfeit miracles, perhaps the best illustration is found in the Old Testament book of Exodus. When Moses and Aaron went to Pharaoh to persuade him to release the children of Israel from bondage, he dismissed them out of hand. Moses instructed Aaron, under the command of God, to take his staff and throw it at Pharaoh's feet (7:9). It immediately "became a serpent" (v. 10).

Pharaoh wasn't impressed. He summoned his "wise men and the sorcerers and they also, the magicians of Egypt, did the same with their secret arts"—their staffs "turned into serpents" (vv. 11–12). Pharaoh ridiculed Moses's and Aaron's God and hardened his heart (v. 13). Not even the fact that "Aaron's staff swallowed up [the magicians'] staffs" (v. 12) convinced Pharaoh to release the Israelites.

A war of wonders ensued. Each time God sent a plague on the Egyptians, the satanic-empowered sorcerers mimicked God's genuine miracle—from turning the Nile into blood (vv. 14–23) to the pestilence of frogs (8:1–7). It looked like Satan was holding his own in a toe-to-toe showdown with the God of the universe.

But that's when God ramped up the miracles. When Moses and Aaron, through the power of God, brought forth lice from the sand of Egypt—and there's a lot of sand in Egypt—Satan's magicians were unable to mimic this miracle. They could only exclaim, "This is the finger of God" (v. 19).

Beware of counterfeit miracles. Just because something looks impressive and inexplicable doesn't automatically mean it's divine; it could be demonic. How do you determine whether a miracle is divine or demonic? You have to examine the person performing the professed miracle.

The Gold Standard for Truth

When it comes to evaluating so-called miracles, there are two critical aspects to look at: the miracle worker's message and his or her motives. One is a *theological test*; the other is a *lifestyle test*.

However, before we dive into either one, we need to agree that the gold standard for all truth is not our experiences, feelings, or the beliefs of a favorite relative. The standard by which we should judge every experience and every teacher is God's Word.

The standard by which we should judge every experience and every teacher is God's Word.

In Acts 17, we find the story of a group of believers who utilized this gold standard for evaluating someone's message. During Paul's second missionary journey, he and Silas traveled to the port town of Thessalonica. However, when the Jews there became outraged at Paul's teaching about Christ, he and Silas fled the city under the cover of darkness and went to the country village of Berea, about forty-five miles southwest of Thessalonica (v. 10).

Their welcome in Berea was as different from their welcome in Thessalonica as a bowl of Häagen-Dazs ice cream is to a bowl of brussels sprouts. The Bereans were "more noble-minded" (v. 11) and received the message of the gospel with grace and "great eagerness" (v. 11). The Bereans were more open-minded than the Thessalonians, but they weren't so open-minded that their brains fell out of their heads. They engaged in "examining the Scriptures daily to see whether these things [Paul and Silas were teaching] were so" (v. 11). The Bereans listened carefully to the evidence presented and then tested those claims against Scripture.

If you're of a certain age and grew up attending Sunday school or vacation Bible school, you know about Bible drills, where the leader calls out an obscure book of the Bible—Zephaniah, let's say—and a chapter and verse. The first contestant to find the correct verse and read it aloud is the winner. I've heard of kids gluing the corners of pages together, like gluing the last page of Habakkuk to the first page of Zephaniah and the last page of Zephaniah to the first page of Haggai, to game the system. Even if you had done that with a Berean, it wouldn't have mattered. They were champions when it came to Bible drills.

But the Bereans didn't just know *where* to find things in their Bible. They *knew* their Bible. Remember, they examined the Scriptures daily. They were students of God's Word, giving it regular attention. They worked hard to understand what God had communicated in His Word and sought to apply it to their everyday lives. They hadn't heard that the long-awaited Messiah had come, that He had died and rose from the dead. So, when Paul and Silas laid out the Old Testament case for Jesus as Messiah, the Bereans, with their knowledge of and desire to obey God's Word, eagerly listened and checked out the claim for themselves.

You must do the same. Don't just accept everything you hear from a preacher as gospel truth just because you like his or her preaching or because he or she performs what appear to be miracles. No. You must be more discerning than that. As a friend said, "Discernment is knowing the difference between a cow patty and a cow patty cookie. They're not the same thing." Theologically speaking, you must be a Berean to know the difference. So, study and apply the Word of God—and use it as the measuring stick against the messages and motives of so-called miracle workers.

The Miracle Worker's Message: The Theological Test

Applying this gold standard for truth to *the theological test*, you need to keep in mind that Satan and his servants rarely, if ever, engage in a frontal assault against your Christian beliefs. They're not likely to tell you to become idolaters and worship other gods (Deut. 13:1–3) or convince you to try divination, contact the dead, or become involved in the occult (18:10–14). They're too clever for that. As masters of disguise—demons masquerading as angels of light—they're going to attack stealthily, with a smile on their faces, to cause you to believe things that just aren't so. The result is the same: you "exchang[e] the truth of God for a lie" (Rom. 1:25). Like the persuasions of an adulteress, the words of false teachers "drip [like] honey" and their speech is "smoother than oil" (Prov. 5:3). Or as Warren Wiersbe put

> **Don't just accept everything you hear from a preacher as gospel truth just because you like his or her preaching or because he or she performs what appear to be miracles.**

it, "False teachers use our vocabulary, but they do not use our dictionary."[4]

False teachers typically concentrate their attacks by using three counterfeit messages. First, *false teachers don't confess Jesus as Christ—the Anointed One*. It's false (and foolish) to believe that every spiritual experience is an experience with the Holy Spirit because there is more than one spirit at work in the world. There is the Spirit of Christ, and there is also the spirit of antichrist. Evidently, some of John's readers fell into the trap of believing theological lies, which prompted the apostle to write pointedly, "Stop it!" That's the Jeffress translation of "Beloved, do not believe every spirit" (1 John 4:1).

False teachers don't confess Jesus as Christ—the Anointed One.

It is important to distinguish the Spirit of Christ from the spirit of antichrist, which John referred to as testing the spirits, because "many false prophets have gone out into the world" (v. 1) to deceive the gullible. The test John applied is a simple one, consisting of two questions. First, does the spirit, or the one who serves as the spirit's mouthpiece, believe that Jesus is the Christ? John wrote, "By this you know the Spirit of God: every spirit that confesses that Jesus Christ . . . is from God" (v. 2). We could read that as, "confess that Jesus *is* the Christ." This is a marker of a true teacher. Failing to confess Jesus as the Christ is the marker of a false teacher, and it leads to the denial of three vital truths:

1. It denies that Jesus is the center of history, the one to whom everything in the past led up to and everything in the present and future looks back upon.
2. It denies that Jesus is the fulfillment of God's promises to redeem sinful people and therefore denies that God can be trusted.
3. It denies that Jesus is God's unique provision for our salvation.[5]

Several years ago, a well-known preacher was interviewed on a nationally televised program. The interviewer asked why he refused to preach on sin or teach that people were under God's judgment if they didn't believe Jesus was the only means of salvation. The pastor answered that it wasn't his place to judge others. Well, that's true in a sense. It isn't his place or my place to judge others by our own arbitrary standards.

However, when we declare that faith in Jesus Christ is the only way to escape an eternity of separation from God, we are not judging others; we are simply repeating a judgment that God has already made. It was Jesus the Son of God who said, "I am the way, and the truth; and the life; no one comes to the Father but through Me" (John 14:6). As my eight-year-old granddaughter explained to me the other night, "Paw-Paw, Jesus didn't say that He was *a way* and *a truth*, but He said He was *the way* and *the truth*." Even an eight-year-old can understand that if we believe Jesus is the Christ, then we must believe everything He says and not hesitate to share His claims about heaven and hell with others.

Here's the second counterfeit message of false teachers: *False teachers don't confess Jesus as coming in the flesh—the incarnation*. This is the second question the apostle John raised in 1 John 4: Does the spirit, or the one who serves as the spirit's mouthpiece, believe Jesus came in the flesh? Picking up with verse 2, "By this you know the Spirit of God: every spirit that confesses that Jesus Christ has come in the flesh is from God." Again, this is a marker of a true teacher. Failing to confess the incarnation is a marker of a false teacher.

Failing to confess the incarnation of Jesus Christ—that He was (and is) fully God *and* fully man—carries with it at least five consequences. If Jesus was not a flesh-and-blood man, He

1. cannot be our example of how to live a life of faith,
2. cannot be our high priest who opens the way to God,
3. cannot be our savior because He cannot identify with those He supposedly came to save,
4. cannot be our resurrection because He could not have died to rise from the dead, body and soul, and
5. cannot be our mediator who stands in the gap between a holy God, who is spirit, and a sinful humanity, who is flesh and spirit, and unites them in holy communion.[6]

Noted atheist Bertrand Russell was once asked, "If God did exist and you were to stand before Him, what would you say to God?" Russell said he would ask God a question: "Sir, why did you not give me better evidence?"[7] If the incarnation of Christ isn't the best evidence of God and His love for sinful humanity, then, as Paul said, we who believe in the incarnation and bodily resurrection of Christ are to be "most . . . pitied" for our "faith is worthless" and we "are still in [our] sins" (1 Cor. 15:19, 17).

Failing to confess Jesus as both Christ and as having come in the flesh leads to the third message espoused by false teachers: *False teachers don't confess Jesus as Lord—the sovereign God*. Paul wrote, "No one speaking by the Holy Spirit of God says, 'Jesus is accursed'; and no one can say, 'Jesus is Lord,' except by the Holy Spirit" (1 Cor. 12:3). "A sneering sinner may mouth the words [Jesus is Lord]," Warren Wiersbe wrote, "but he is not giving a true confession."[8]

If Jesus isn't God, there are three tragic consequences for all humanity:

1. If Jesus isn't God, He couldn't have been a sinless man.
2. If Jesus wasn't a sinless man, His death on the cross was insufficient to pay the divine debt of sin.
3. If Jesus's death on the cross was insufficient to pay the divine debt of sin, His bones are still buried in His grave . . . and you and I will remain in the grave, as well.

If these facts are true, you and I—and everyone who's placed their faith in Christ through the generations—are "more to be pitied than anyone in the world" (1 Cor. 15:19 NLT). Yet by the power of the Holy Spirit, we claim with full confidence, "Jesus is Lord!"

Some years ago, Christian philosopher Peter Kreeft wrote,

> If you confess at a fashionable cocktail party that you personally love to play with porcupines, or plan to sell CIA secrets to the communists, or that you are considering becoming a Palestinian terrorist, you will find a buzzing, fascinated crowd around you, eager to listen. But if you confess that you believe that Jesus Christ is God, that he died to save us from sin, or that there really are a Heaven and a Hell, you will very soon be talking to empty air, with a distinct chill in it.[9]

Although embracing those core beliefs will not make you popular, espousing them without apology is the duty and privilege of every Christian.

In my experience through the years, I've discovered that false teachers don't necessarily tip their hand so easily by denying Christ outright. Rather, they masquerade their lies as truth by failing to affirm Christ clearly. More often than not, heresies creep into the church through the conscious decision of false teachers to steer away from important biblical doctrines like Jesus's messiahship, His incarnation, and His lordship.

One last word before moving on to evaluating false teachers' motives. We judge the spirits (and the mouthpieces of the spirits) *not by their works*, which can appear to be spectacular, but *by their words*.

Jesus warned His disciples, "Beware of false prophets, who come to you in sheep's clothing, but inwardly are ravenous wolves" (Matt. 7:15). He then said, "You will know them by their fruits" (v. 16). Don't think of "fruit" in this context as something manifested physically, like a miracle. That's not what Jesus meant, as He made clear later when He linked "fruit" with speech:

> Either make the tree good and its fruit good, or make the tree bad and its fruit bad; for the tree is known by its fruit. You brood of vipers, how can you, being evil, speak what is good? For the mouth speaks out of that which fills the heart. The good man brings out of his good treasure what is good; and the evil man brings out of his evil treasure what is evil. But I tell you that every careless word that people speak, they shall give an accounting for it in the day of judgment. (12:33–36)

It's not the *miracle* that sets the false teacher apart from the true teacher; it's the *message*. Beware of counterfeit messages that water down the gospel of Jesus Christ and fail to confess His humanity and His deity.

The Miracle Worker's Motive: The Lifestyle Test

You've learned to apply the discernment test to so-called miracles by evaluating the person's *message*. Now, you need to learn how to apply the discernment test to their *motives*. Godly teachers glorify Christ by communicating an undefiled message and serving others. That's what motivates them. Ungodly teachers, on the other hand, are motivated by two other considerations, broadly speaking.

First, *ungodly teachers seek to satisfy their flesh.* Jude wrote of them, "For certain persons have crept in unnoticed"—that is, they've wormed their way through theological cracks—and called them "ungodly persons who turn the grace of our God into licentiousness and deny our only Master and Lord, Jesus Christ" (v. 4). Peter echoed Jude's insight into what motivates false teachers, but he added a note about their attractiveness: "Many will follow their sensuality" (2 Pet. 2:2).

Make no mistake, false teachers usually possess a charismatic personality. But don't confuse charisma with character. As Christian philosopher Os Guinness points out, "Charisma without character is dangerous and manipulative."[10]

These preachers pronounce a squishy theology—one that looks the other way at sexual sin. Sloppy doctrine often leads to sensual decadence. When people abandon God's standard of truth, they also abandon His standard of morality in favor of a worldly morality. My seminary professor and mentor Howard Hendricks used to say, "We walk down the road of immorality when we walk away from God's Word." And since indecency appeals to the flesh, many follow the example of false teachers, justifying their own indecency because the indecency of their teachers gives them cover. But immorality dressed up in spiritual garb is nothing more than a corpse with lipstick.

Of course, the disconnect between the motives and the sometimes orthodox messages of false teachers leads to hypocrisy, which Os Guinness defined as "a lie told in deeds rather than words."[11] Jude called such teachers "worldly-minded, devoid of the Spirit [of God]." As a result, they "cause divisions" among believers (v. 19). And they cause derision among unbelievers, who look at these supposed Christian teachers who can't distinguish between the worldly and the heavenly—and sneer.

Make no mistake, false teachers usually possess a charismatic personality. But don't confuse charisma with character.

I don't need to recount to you all the sexual scandals that have stained the church in recent decades. No wonder Peter concluded that because of false teachers who are motivated by their lusts, "the way of the truth [is] maligned" (2 Pet. 2:2). And because that's true, Jude concluded such teachers have been "marked out for . . . condemnation" (v. 4).

Second, *ungodly teachers seek to satisfy their greed.* False teachers are not only motivated by the "lust of the flesh," as John put it, but they're also motivated by the "lust of the eyes" (1 John 2:16). Peter wrote, "In their greed they will exploit you with false words" (2 Pet. 2:3). Their eyes turn green with envy if they see anyone with more than they have. To satisfy themselves, they use rubber words—words that can be twisted and shaped, molded into whatever meaning they want—to persuade gullible people out of their money.[12]

You've probably seen television preachers pleading for funds in exchange for prayers or miracles or selling handkerchiefs with the preacher's sweat that will cure all sorts of diseases—for a price, always for a price—to enrich themselves.

Jesus didn't do that. Nor did His apostles. John the Baptist dressed in camel hair and ate locusts and wild honey. Jesus was virtually homeless, with "nowhere to lay His head" (Matt. 8:20). I'm not saying preachers must live like paupers. But when a minister says the Lord told him to ask you for your hard-earned money so he can purchase a new airplane—for the sake of the ministry, no doubt—then your Berean instincts should kick in.

In the Old Testament book of Micah, the Lord condemned Israel's political and religious leaders for being motivated by personal gain rather than the people's good. They "pronounce judgment for a bribe, her priests instruct for a price and her prophets divine for money" (3:11). One example of this was Gehazi, the prophet Elisha's understudy, who sacrificed his calling as a prophet for the calling of profit.[13]

False teachers like Gehazi—or the Pharisees of Jesus's time, or the false prophets of Peter's and Jude's day, or the charlatans of today—are motivated by the same pursuits: to "[follow] after their own lusts" and to "speak . . . flattering [words] for the sake of gaining an advantage" over others (Jude 16). Though they may be charismatic and attractive, just as Satan is when he masquerades as an angel of light, men and women like this are nothing but "whitewashed tombs which on the outside appear beautiful, but inside . . . are full of dead men's bones and all uncleanness . . . full of hypocrisy and lawlessness" (Matt. 23:27–28).

Of all the indictments against counterfeit Christian preachers and performers of miracles, Jude 12–13 levels the greatest:

> These people are eyesores at your love feasts as you worship and eat together. They're giving you a black eye—carousing shamelessly, grabbing anything that isn't nailed down. They're—
>
> Puffs of smoke pushed by gusts of wind;
> late autumn trees stripped clean of leaf and fruit,
> Doubly dead, pulled up by the roots;
> wild ocean waves leaving nothing on the beach
> but the foam of their shame;
> Lost stars in outer space
> on their way to the black hole. (MSG)

When evaluating those who claim to be miracle workers or miracle recipients, be a Berean and beware of counterfeit messages and counterfeit motives.

CONCLUSION

YOUR DIVINE INVITATION

SWAN QUARTER, NORTH CAROLINA, is an area that is prone to flooding, especially when a hurricane blows through. That's why members of Methodist Episcopal Church South approached Sam Sadler about purchasing a high-lying lot he owned in the center of town for their new sanctuary. He told them no. Then he added it would take a miracle for him to sell that lot to the church.

Disappointed, the congregation continued to look for a place to build. One day, James Hayes knocked on their door. He had a lot that he would gift to the congregation. It wasn't a prime location, certainly not compared to Mr. Sadler's lot, but it was free. The congregation praised God and began construction, starting with brick piers, on which they built a modest wooden sanctuary.

On September 16, 1876, on the eve of dedicating their new church building, a storm blew in off the North Carolina coast. The wind whipped, the rain poured, and the surf crashed on the beaches. As the day wore on, the wind became stronger, the rain became heavier, and the surf became rougher. The storm intensified overnight. By the dawn of September 17, a tidal surge had reached Swan Quarter. Creeks overflowed their banks. And the little Methodist church building became unmoored from its brick pylons and floated away.

The wooden sanctuary drifted down Oyster Creek Road, bumped into George Credle's general store, took a sharp right turn, and headed down Main Street for two blocks until it reached Church Street, where it turned left, crossed the Carawan canal, and came to rest on some high ground—right in the middle of Mr. Sadler's property. The waters had barely subsided from Swan Quarter when Mr. Sadler sold the lot to the congregation of the Methodist Episcopal Church, which they renamed Providence Methodist Church—the church, as its historical marker says, that was "moved by the hand of God."[1]

We've looked at miracles of power, provision, protection, and healing. Through it all, my prayer has been that the *Worker* of miracles has made a greater impression on your heart and mind than the *works* of miracles. After all, the purpose of every miracle is to focus our attention on the one true Miracle Worker, not on the miracle worked.

Now that you've reached the end of this book on miracles, the only question worth asking and answering is this: *Have you been moved by the hand of God?* If you're a believer in the Lord Jesus Christ, has something in this book encouraged you to draw closer to the Miracle Worker—to remain more faithful to Him and to offer greater heartfelt praise for His divine invasions in your life?

If you've struggled to believe, what has piqued your curiosity about the miracle-working God? Would it surprise you to learn that He wants to perform the greatest miracle of all in your life today? He does.

Without the miracle of the incarnation, the miracle of Jesus paying for your sins on the cross couldn't and didn't happen. His death would mean nothing more than another first-century Jew being crucified by Roman soldiers.

Equally true, without the miracle of the incarnation, the miracle of Jesus's resurrection couldn't and didn't happen. The story of His resurrection from the dead would just be another religious myth.

But those miracles *did* happen. Jesus's death did pay for your sins, and Jesus's resurrection was proof that God accepted that payment. The question is, Will you be moved by the hand of God and believe that the Worker of miracles offers you the greatest miracle of all—eternal salvation?

Will you be moved by the hand of God and believe that the Worker of miracles offers you the greatest miracle of all—eternal salvation?

God invites you to move from a life of guilt and shame to a life of freedom and joy, to move from an eternity spent in hell apart from the God who loves you to an eternity spent in heaven united with the God who loves you.

If you're seeking a divine invasion in your life, the place to begin is in accepting His divine invitation for you to enter a new life. Paul wrote, "If you confess with your mouth Jesus as Lord, and believe in your heart that God raised Him from the dead, you will be saved; for with the heart a person believes, resulting in righteousness, and with the mouth he confesses, resulting in salvation" (Rom. 10:9–10).

Have you been moved by the hand of God? Would you like to receive God's forgiveness and know for sure that one day you will be welcomed into heaven? If so, you can accept the divine invitation He's extending to you right now by saying a prayer that goes something like this, knowing that God is listening:

> *Dear God, thank You for loving me. I know that I have failed You in so many ways, and I'm truly sorry for the sins in my life. I believe that You love me so much that You gave Your Son, Jesus, to die on the cross for me, to take the punishment I deserve to take for my sins. Right now, I'm trusting in what Jesus did for me—not in my good works—to save me from my sins. Thank You for forgiving me, and help me to live the rest of my life for You. In Jesus's name, amen.*

Accepting God's invitation to eternal life is the only means for a divine invasion—the greatest miracle of all: your salvation.

NOTES

Chapter 1 Divine Invasions

1. W. A. Criswell, "The Seven Tests of Faith," sermon, May 15, 1960, W. A. Criswell Sermon Library, https://wacriswell.com/sermons/1960/the-seven-tests-of-faith.

2. Robert Jeffress, *Courageous: 10 Strategies for Thriving in a Hostile World* (Baker Books, 2020), 105–7.

3. The seven "signs" of Jesus recorded in the Gospel of John are turning water into wine at Cana (2:1–11); healing an official's son in Capernaum (4:46–54); healing an infirm man at the Pool of Bethesda (5:1–15); feeding the five thousand near Bethsaida (6:1–14); walking on water at the Sea of Galilee (John 6:6–21); healing a man born blind at Jerusalem (9:1–7); and raising Lazarus from the dead at Bethany (11:14–44; 12:18).

4. Many of these same miracles were performed by the apostles after Jesus's ascension. But it should be noted the apostles performed these miracles in the name and through the power of Jesus.

5. *Love and Death*, written and directed by Woody Allen (United Artists, 1975), www.imdb.com/title/tt0073312/characters/nm0000095/.

Chapter 2 Miracles of Power

1. Billy Graham, *Just As I Am: The Autobiography of Billy Graham* (HarperOne, 2024), 139.

2. Émile Souvestre, *Les Derniers Bretons* (*The Last Bretons*), vol. 1 (Charpentier, Libraire-Editeur, 1836), 121.

3. Larry Richards divides these clusters into broad categories he calls "*authenticating* miracles," which validate a new message from God and His messenger, and "*supportive* miracles," which reinforce God's message and messenger to a new generation. See Larry Richards, *Every Miracle and Wonder in the Bible* (Thomas Nelson, 1998), 285; emphasis in original.

4. See Ron Rhodes, "Notable Apostolic Miracles," in *Miracles Around Us: How to Recognize God at Work Today* (Harvest House, 2000), 127–28.

5. Jewish prayer from the time of the Maccabees, as quoted in Os Guinness, *Carpe Diem Redeemed: Seizing the Day, Discerning the Time* (InterVarsity, 2019), 87.

6. *Omnipotent* is a compound word from the Latin *omni*, "all," and *potent*, "powerful."

7. Craig S. Keener has collected many stories of modern-day miracles from around the world. See Craig S. Keener, *Miracles Today: The Supernatural Work of God in the Modern World* (Baker Academic, 2021).

8. Peter Kreeft, *Back to Virtue: Traditional Moral Wisdom for Modern Moral Confusion* (Ignatius Press, 1992), 105.

9. Thomas L. Constable, "Notes on Isaiah: 2025 Edition," pdf, accessed November 11, 2025, https://soniclight.com/tcon/notes/pdf/isaiah.pdf, 274.

10. For Scriptures about God's power, see Gen. 18:14; Job 42:2; Jer. 32:17, 27; Zech. 8:6; Matt. 19:26; Mark 10:27; Luke 1:37; 18:27.

11. Lucius Annaeus Seneca, "Letters, LXXIII," *Sentences from Seneca*, trans. Dana Gioia (Trinity Forum, 2023), 35.

12. In Ephesians 5:18, the Greek verb translated as "be filled" (*plerousthe*) is in the present tense and could be translated "Be filled continually." It's possible to be filled with the Spirit on Sunday and not on Monday.

13. Derrick G. Jeter, *Paul's Swan Song: A Study of 2 Timothy* (IFL Publishing House, 2015), 138.

14. Karl Barth, as quoted in Philip Yancey, *Prayer: Does It Make Any Difference?* (Zondervan, 2006), 118.

Chapter 3 Miracles of Provision

1. Adlai E. Stevenson, "Social Gains and the Public Welfare," speech at Franklin County Memorial Auditorium, Columbus, Ohio,

October 3, 1952, in *Major Campaign Speeches of Adlai E. Stevenson, 1952* (Random House, 1953), 200.

2. I wrote at length about these needs in *18 Minutes with Jesus: Straight Talk from the Savior about the Things That Matter Most* (Baker Books, 2022), 171–76.

3. Ralph Waldo Emerson, "We Thank Thee," in Franklin B. Dyer and Mary J. Brady, *Fourth Reader* (Charles E. Merrill, 1916), 35.

4. Gary Portnoy and Judy Hart Angelo, "Where Everybody Knows Your Name: Theme from *Cheers*," in *Vocal Popular Sheet Music Collection*, score 5142 (Addax Music Co., 1982), https://digitalcommons.library.umaine.edu/mmb-vp-copyright/5142.

5. Robert Jeffress, *Invincible: Conquering the Mountains That Separate You from the Blessed Life* (Baker Books, 2021), 165.

6. See "The State of Church Attendance: Trends and Statistics [2025]," Churchtrac, accessed November 11, 2025, www.churchtrac.com/articles/the-state-of-church-attendance-trends-and-statistics-2023; Jeffrey M. Jones, "U.S. Church Attendance Still Lower than Pre-Pandemic," Gallup, June 26, 2023, https://news.gallup.com/poll/507692/church-attendance-lower-pre-pandemic.aspx#.

7. The title "A Psalm of Praise, of David" in Psalm 145 is unique. It only occurs here in the book of Psalms but is also repetitive and states the obvious. By their very nature, psalms are songs of praise. As Augustine wrote, "Psalms are the praises of God accompanied with song; psalms are songs containing the praise of God. If there be praise, but not of God, it is not a psalm. If there be praise, and praise of God, if it is not sung, it is not a psalm. To make a psalm there go these three—praise, God's praise, and song." As quoted in Charles Haddon Spurgeon, *The Treasury of David*, vol. 7 (London: Passmore and Alabaster, 1886), 381.

8. Warren W. Wiersbe, "Psalms," in *The Wiersbe Bible Commentary: The Complete Old Testament in One Volume* (David C. Cook, 2007), 1045–46.

9. J. Vernon McGee, *Second Corinthians*, Thru the Bible Commentary series (Thomas Nelson, 1991), 114.

10. The title to Psalm 34 summarizes the historical background but mentions Abimelech, not Achish. Abimelech might have been a title for all the kings of Gath, of which Achish was at the time David arrived in Gath, or Abimelech might be the Semitic name for the Philistine Achish. See Thomas L. Constable, "Notes on Psalms: 2025 Edition," pdf, accessed November 11, 2025, https://soniclight.com/tcon/notes/pdf/psalms.pdf, 172.

11. To read more of Julia's story, see Julia Jeffress Sadler, *Pray Big Things: The Surprising Life God Has for You When You're Bold Enough to Ask* (Baker Books, 2019).

Chapter 4 Miracles of Protection

1. Havelock Ellis, *Little Essays of Love and Virtue* (George H. Doran, 1922), 100.
2. See Ps. 33:6; 89:11–13; 96:4–5; 104:2–9; 115:15; 124:8; 134:3; 136:4–9.
3. See Ps. 31:8; 56:13; 66:9; 125:1; Prov. 2:8; 3:23, 23, 25–26.
4. Donald Grey Barnhouse, "God's Providence," in *Romans, vol. 7: God's Heirs* (repr. 2023: Eerdmans, 1963), chapter XIV.
5. Wiersbe, "Psalms," *Wiersbe Bible Commentary: Complete Old Testament*, 1022.
6. Derrick G. Jeter, "Goodbye to a River," *Y'allogy*, November 12, 2021, www.yallogy.com/p/goodbye-to-a-river. Quoted by permission.
7. David Jeremiah (@davidjeremiah), "If you are fearful remember: God's man in the center of God's will is immortal," Twitter post, January 27, 2014, https://x.com/davidjeremiah/status/427912875618082817. He also quotes this with slight variations, and indicates an unnamed friend gave him a note with the quote on it, in *Prayer, the Great Adventure* (Multnomah, 1997), 218.
8. Tim Hawkins, *Diary of a Jackwagon* (Nelson, 2015), 51.
9. See Ps. 18:2; 19:14; 62:2, 6; 71:3; 78:35; 94:22; 95:1.
10. Adapted from Billy Graham, *Angels: God's Secret Agents* (W Publishing, 1995), 3–4.
11. Thomas Watson, as quoted in Warren W. Wiersbe, "Acts," in *The Wiersbe Bible Commentary: The Complete New Testament in One Volume* (David C. Cook, 2007), 362.
12. See John 15:26–27; 16:7; Acts 1:6, 8; 2:1–4.
13. William Barclay, *The Gospel of John, Volume 2*, The New Daily Study Bible series (Westminster John Knox, 2017), 194; emphasis in original.

Chapter 5 Miracles of Healing

1. Lee Strobel interview with Roger E. Olson, in *The Case for Miracles: A Journalist Investigates Evidence for the Supernatural* (Zondervan, 2018), 219–20.

2. "United States Wellness Economy Now Valued at $1.8 Trillion—The Largest Wellness Market in the World," Global Wellness Institute, April 17, 2024, https://globalwellnessinstitute.org/press-room/press-releases/united-states-wellness-economy-now-valued-at-1-8-trillion-the-largest-wellness-market-in-the-world/.

3. Adapted from David Jeremiah, *Searching for Heaven on Earth: How to Find What Really Matters in Life* (Integrity, 2004), 298.

4. Benjamin Franklin, "Letter to Jean-Baptiste Le Roy, November 13, 1789," in *The Works of Benjamin Franklin*, vol. 10, ed. Jared Sparks (Philadelphia: Childs & Peterson, 1840), 410.

5. "O Worship the King, All Glorious Above," lyrics by Robert Grant (1833), public domain.

6. Nathaniel Hawthorne, *The Scarlet Letter* (Barnes & Noble, 2011), 118.

7. Jordan S. Rubin, *The Maker's Diet* (Penguin, 2004), 158.

8. See John 5:19, 30; 8:28; 12:49; 14:10.

9. See also Isa. 30:26.

10. Frederick William Danker, ed., *A Greek-English Lexicon of the New Testament and Other Early Christian Literature*, 3rd rev. ed. (University of Chicago Press, 2000), 871.

11. See Matt. 4:2; John 4:6; 6:15; 19:28.

12. Chip Schweiger, "Cowboy Coffee: The Strongest Brew on the Open Range," *Way Out West* podcast, March 18, 2025, https://podcast.ridewayoutwest.com/cowboycoffee/.

13. See Eric J. Olson, "How Many Hours of Sleep Are Enough for Good Health?," Mayo Clinic, accessed November 10, 2025, www.mayoclinic.org/healthy-lifestyle/adult-health/expert-answers/how-many-hours-of-sleep-are-enough/faq-20057898.

14. See Matt. 14:13; Mark 1:35; Luke 4:42; 6:12.

15. Joni Eareckson Tada, "Why Joni Eareckson Tada Praises God for Not Healing Her," The Gospel Coalition, July 17, 2019, www.thegospelcoalition.org/article/joni-earekson-tada-praises-healing/.

Chapter 6 When Your Miracle Doesn't Come

1. Unless otherwise noted, all quotations from Douglas Groothuis are from an interview with Lee Strobel in *The Case for Miracles: A Journalist Investigates Evidence for the Supernatural* (Zondervan, 2018), 241–44.

2. Douglas Groothuis, *Walking Through Twilight: A Wife's Illness—A Philosopher's Lament* (InterVarsity, 2017), 162.

3. John Wesley, *The Nature of Spiritual Growth* (Bethany House, 1987), 33.

4. Oswald Chambers, "Facing Reality," in *The Quotable Oswald Chambers*, ed. David McCasland (Discovery House, 2008), 93.

5. Adapted from Henry W. Holloman, "Sanctification: Rediscovering the Transforming Power of Sanctification," in *Understanding Christian Theology*, ed. Charles R. Swindoll and Roy B. Zuck (Thomas Nelson, 2003), 1035–39.

6. Commentators have speculated on what Paul's "thorn in the flesh" was, proposing poor eyesight or arthritis (Gal. 6:11), a speech impediment (1 Cor. 2:1), malaria, or epilepsy (Gal. 4:13–15).

7. Charles Haddon Spurgeon, *An All-Round Ministry: Direction, Wisdom, and Encouragement for Preacher and Pastors* (Banner of Truth Trust, 1972), 384.

8. Wiersbe, "2 Corinthians," *Wiersbe Bible Commentary: Complete New Testament*, 540; emphasis in original.

9. Wiersbe, "2 Corinthians," *Wiersbe Bible Commentary: Complete New Testament*, 540.

10. George Müller, *The Life of Trust: Being a Narrative of the Lord's Dealings* (Gould and Lincoln, 1868), 243.

11. Charles R. Swindoll, *Strengthen Your Grip: Essentials in an Aimless World* (Word, 1982), 206–7.

12. Lloyd John Ogilvie, as quoted in R. Kent Hughes, *James: Faith That Works*, Preaching the Word series (Crossway, 1991), 18.

13. Adapted from Abderrahim El Makkouri, in Richard Hamilton, *The Last Storytellers: Tales from the Heart of Morocco* (L. B. Tauris & Co. Ltd., 2011), 36–37.

14. Adrian Rogers, *Believe in Miracles but Trust in Jesus* (Crossway, 1997), 13.

15. Aleksandr I. Solzhenitsyn, *The Gulag Archipelago, 1919–1956: An Experiment in Literary Investigation, III–IV*, vol. 2, trans. Thomas P. Whitney (Harper & Row, 1975), 615, 616–17.

16. See John 14:16, 26; 15:26; 16:7.

Chapter 7 Beware of Counterfeit Miracles

1. For Satan's power over *humans*, see Luke 13:11, 16; Acts 10:38; 16:16; for *governments*, see Matt. 4:8–9; 2 Cor. 4:4; for *angels*, see Eph. 6:11–12; Jude 9; and for *religion*, see Rev. 2:9; 3:9.

2. G. K. Chesterton, *Saint Thomas Aquinas: "The Dumb Ox"* (Image Books, 2001), 68.

3. Adapted from Ron Rhodes, *Miracles Around Us: How to Recognize God at Work Today* (Harvest House, 2000), 208–9.

4. Wiersbe, "2 Peter," *Wiersbe Bible Commentary: Complete New Testament*, 938.

5. See William Barclay, *The Letters of John and Jude*, The New Daily Study Bible series (Westminster John Knox, 2017), 104–5.

6. See Barclay, *Letters of John and Jude*, 105–6.

7. Bertrand Russell, as quoted in Leo Rosten, "Bertrand Russell and God: A Memoir," *The Saturday Review* (February 23, 1976), 26.

8. Wiersbe, "1 Corinthians," *Wiersbe Bible Commentary: Complete New Testament*, 485.

9. Peter Kreeft, *Back to Virtue: Traditional Moral Wisdom for Modern Moral Confusion* (Ignatius Press, 1992), 30.

10. Os Guinness, *When No One Sees: The Importance of Character in an Age of Image* (NavPress, 2000), 40.

11. Os Guinness, *Fool's Talk: Recovering the Art of Christian Persuasion* (InterVarsity, 2015), 195.

12. The Greek word translated as "false" in 2 Peter 2:3 is *plastos*, from which we get the English word *plastic*.

13. See 2 Kings 5:1–27.

Conclusion: Your Divine Invitation

1. Adapted from "Moved by the Hand of God," September 21, 2021, North Carolina Conference of the United Methodist Church, https://nccumc.org/history/2021/09/moved-by-the-hand-of-god/; Connie Leinbach, "Legend Lives on of Church 'Moved by Hand of God,'" *The Daily Advance*, December 28, 2023, www.dailyadvance.com/features/local/legend-lives-on-of-church-moved-by-hand-of-god/article_973dfec4-a509-11ee-9b31-6ff9b9116e69.html.

ABOUT THE AUTHOR

Dr. Robert Jeffress is senior pastor of the sixteen-thousand-member First Baptist Church, Dallas, Texas. Located in the heart of downtown, First Baptist Dallas is built on the Bible and has been reaching the city, nation, and world for Jesus Christ for more than 150 years. Led by Dr. Jeffress since 2007, the church completed a $130 million renovation and expansion in 2013 and now occupies six city blocks—enhancing the church's ability to carry out its mission of transforming the world with God's Word . . . one life at a time.

Dr. Jeffress is a FOX News contributor and appears regularly on FOX News Channel's *FOX & Friends*, *FOX News @ Night*, *Hannity*, and *The Faulkner Focus* and on the FOX Business Network. Dr. Jeffress has made more than four thousand guest appearances on television programs that include HBO's *Real Time with Bill Maher* and Trinity Broadcasting Network's *Praise*.

Established in 1996, *Pathway to Victory* serves as the broadcast ministry of Dr. Jeffress and exists to pierce the darkness with the light of God's Word through the most effective media available. The daily radio program airs on more than one thousand stations, and in 2025 the

National Religious Broadcasters Association recognized *Pathway to Victory* with its prestigious Radio Program of the Year award. The daily television program can be seen on over eleven thousand cable and satellite systems, including Trinity Broadcasting Network (TBN), where it has been the number one most-watched program since 2020. *Pathway to Victory* broadcasts are translated into six languages and reach 193 countries throughout the world in addition to all major markets in the USA. On each daily broadcast, Dr. Jeffress provides practical application of God's Word to everyday life through clear, uncompromised biblical teaching. Additionally, *Pathway to Victory* ministers globally through podcasting, social media, and other digital media.

Dr. Jeffress is the author of more than forty books, including *Not All Roads Lead to Heaven*, *A Place Called Heaven*, *Choosing the Extraordinary Life*, *Courageous*, *Invincible*, *18 Minutes with Jesus*, *What Every Christian Should Know*, *The 10*, and *Jesus Revealed in the End Times*.

Dr. Jeffress graduated with a DMin from Southwestern Baptist Theological Seminary, a ThM from Dallas Theological Seminary, and a BS from Baylor University. He was awarded a Doctor of Divinity degree from Dallas Baptist University and received the Distinguished Alumnus of the Year award from Southwestern Baptist Theological Seminary. He is also an adjunct professor at Dallas Theological Seminary.

Dr. Jeffress and his wife, Amy, have two daughters and three grandchildren.